Patio Gardening

by
Jack Kramer

Photos: Jerry Bagger, Matthew Barr, Roger Scharmer

Published by HPBooks, a division of Price Stern Sloan, Inc.
360 North La Cienega Boulevard
Los Angeles, CA 90048
ISBN 0-89586-033-3
Library of Congress Catalog Card Number 80-80018
©1983 Fisher Publishing, Inc.
Printed in U.S.A.
9 8 7 6 5 4
Previously published under the title, Gardening in Small Spaces.

Table of Contents

Your Small Space
1

BIG GARDENS IN LITTLE PLACES

If you do not have enough space for the garden of your dreams, you can still have a very lovely garden in the tiniest area. You can grow plants in terraced beds or on trellises or in a vertical post garden. Or plant your garden in a corner. If you have no land at all, consider a charming porch or rooftop garden. A garden in the air can delight the eye and you can grow almost any plant you want. If you are city bound, don't give up a garden—even the smallest backyard or sideyard can become a handsome setting. So can a small entrance garden.

All space-saving gardening requires is careful planning and some construction. The garden plans in this book are designed to get the most from the smallest piece of land. You will find space saving plans and working construction drawings for all kinds of gardens. If it is a garden you want, you can have it—and now!

Also included is a complete discussion about plants for your gardens—how to select them and how to grow them for maximum beauty.

SPACE-SAVING GARDENS

Most of us think of a garden as a large expanse of flowers and greenery, rather like a gracious English Manor garden. Yet a garden can be very small and still productive and quite pretty. And concentrating the plants in one small area makes watering and caring for plants easy work. You can grow almost anything if you know how to plan and arrange the garden in a small backyard, on a porch or rooftop, or in an atrium or entranceway. It all boils down to maximum use of minimum space. No longer do you have to shy away from growing the plants you've always wanted—anyone, in almost any sized space, can enjoy the benefits and pleasures of a garden.

ADVANTAGES

Gardening in a small area does not mean less work or less of a garden. A small garden can have distinct advantages. For one thing, watering is simpler in a small garden — you *control* rather than waste the water. And you don't have plants scattered here and there throughout large grounds that never get watered or cared for.

Gardening on a small scale also provides you with another advantage: the chance to take a closer look at your plants. Observation is necessary for good gardening; you must detect insects before they become monster colonies, and you should look at and know your plants. You can learn to tell a healthy plant from an unhealthy one just by looking at leaves and stems. Healthy plants are firm and perky, not wilted or weak.

In a large garden you may forget where you planted bulbs or which vegetable is which, but not in the small garden. You know exactly where everything is. You can be more productive and more organized, and bring more beauty to your outdoor area. Garden catalogs picture beautiful large flower gardens with an orchard in one spot and vegetables in another. This is fine for people who can afford gardeners or the time to care for their plants. But a small garden is the intelligent answer for people with limited time or space. You have control, you care and tend, gather and nurture, and you experience the infinite pleasure of seeing things prosper.

Finally, a small garden has the very important advantage of being less strain on your budget. You do not need truckloads of soil or copious amounts of fertilizer and plant materials.

HOW TO PLAN A GARDEN

PLOT EXISTING ELEMENTS ON GRAPH PAPER

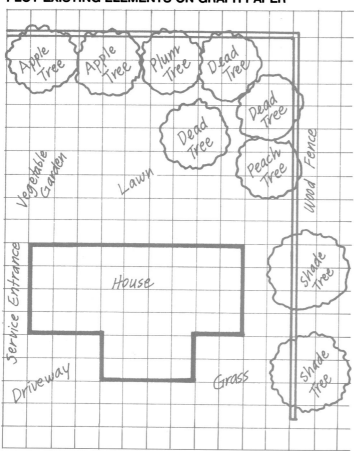

PLOT LIVING AREAS DESIRED AND GROWING CONDITIONS

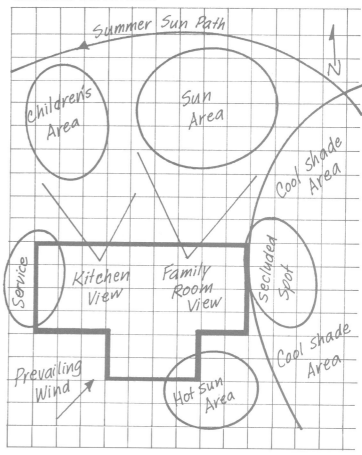

WHAT YOU CAN GROW

You can actually grow almost anything you want: perennials and annuals in a cutting garden, bountiful vegetables, even fruit trees if you *espalier* them, that is train them to grow flat on a fence or trellis. You can even have three gardens in a small area. The key to success is careful planning and providing proper growing conditions. Find out the correct planting times and exposure, soil and water requirements before you plant.

I combine vegetables, flowers, berries and four espaliered fruit trees in my 10 x 20-foot garden. However, I grow most of my garden on vertical supports, which make plants easier to see and reach.

PLANNING

First, look around and decide what area the garden will occupy. Look for a good sunny spot because most flowers and vegetables need at least 4 hours of sun a day. A western, eastern or southern exposure is what you want. Consider porches and garage roofs. These can carry spectacular gardens. Even the smallest home has some space in back, in front or at the side. This space can be a productive garden.

Walk the area off and count the footage, just as you do when measuring a room. Count each step you take as 1 foot. Be sure you consider all your space. Sideyards are often overlooked, as are vertical spaces along fences.

DEVELOP GENERAL IDEAS

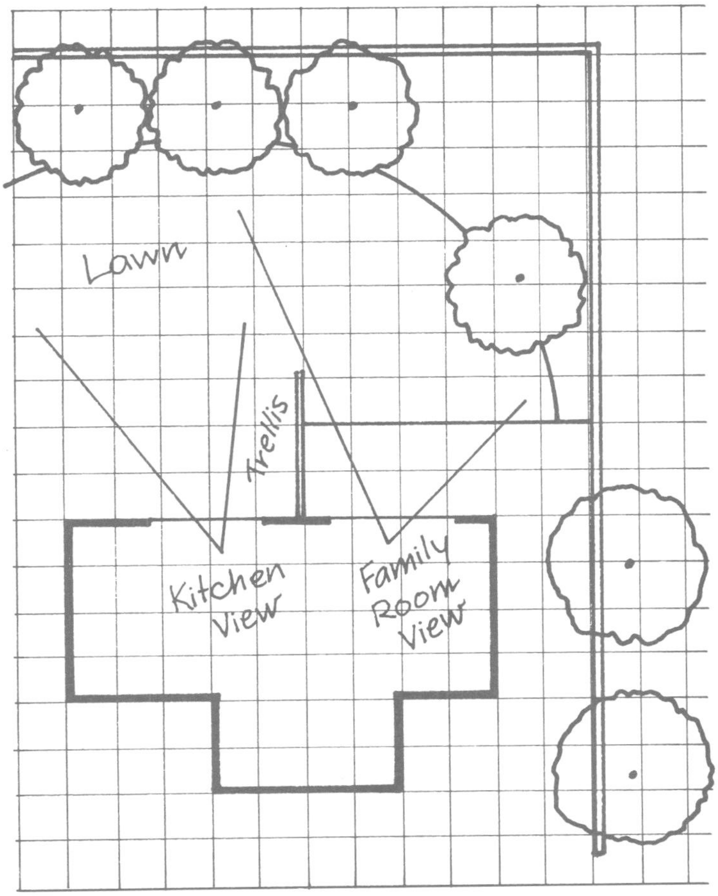

Lawn

Trellis

Kitchen View

Family Room View

FINISH PLAN

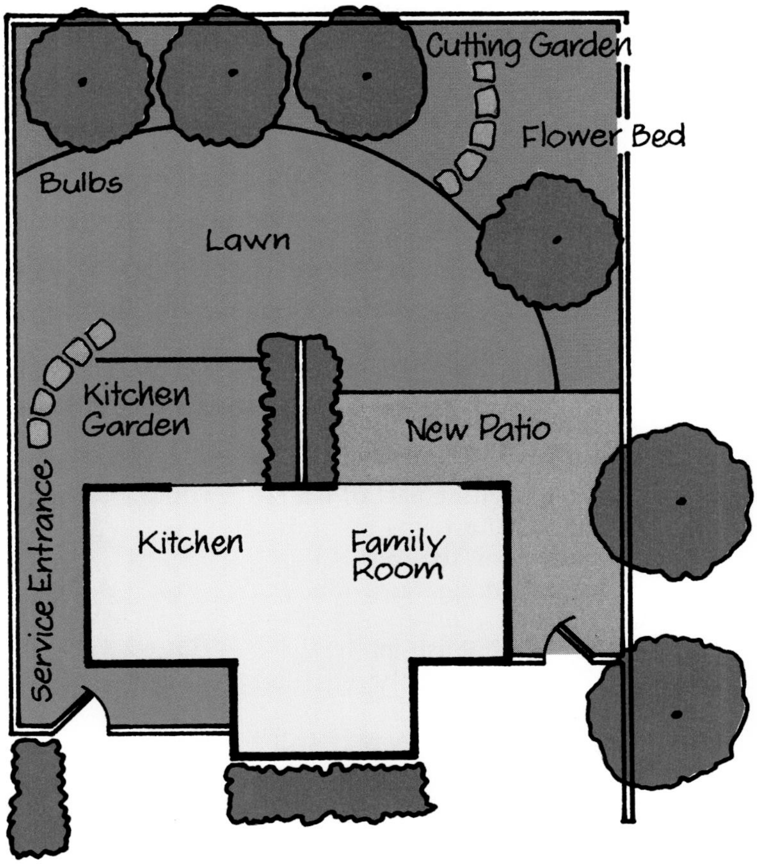

Cutting Garden

Flower Bed

Bulbs

Lawn

Service Entrance

Kitchen Garden

New Patio

Kitchen

Family Room

It is essential to make a plan of your garden. Now, don't say you can't draw so you can't plan. You don't have to draw—just sketch what you want. Think in terms of how you want to use your garden. Do you want to raise fruits or vegetables? Do you want a beautiful, private place to sit or look at from your home? Do you want cutting flowers to take inside? Or do you want a spa or hot tub to relax in?

Color in the planting areas, including any containers you plan to use. This will help you decide how much construction will be needed. This will also give you a rough idea of how many plants you want. Even from this sketchy picture you will get an idea of scale and unity. The

drawings on these pages will give you some suggestions for making your plan.

SCALE, PROPORTION, UNITY AND RHYTHM

Plants have definite forms. They are spreading or horizontal, round or globular, weeping or trailing, and vertical—pyramidal—or columnar in shape. Dogwood, pin oak and hawthorn have strong horizontal lines and carry the eye from one plant to another. These are good selections for low flat houses. Beech, flowering cherry and weeping willow are delicate and fragile in appearance and create softer lines. They are best displayed in front of stiffer-looking subjects.

The form of a plant is vitally important in landscaping. Unless you know what the plant will look like when it is mature, selecting form becomes a guessing game. When you make selections, try to visualize the fully grown plant. Some species lose their symmetrical form with age. Others, like pines and some firs, lose their lower branches as they get older. The photos in this book were chosen to help you visualize common plants.

Scale and proportion must be carefully considered in landscaping because they are the keys to an attractive setting.

Scale: A Relationship of Size—Creating an illusion of space with plant materials is an exciting part of landscaping. Scale is the visual relationship of each form to every other form and to the design as a whole. It can be called a relationship of size. You must establish an appealing scale relationship between the garden and the house. The starting point can be a large tree that will link the house and the garden together; it will be part of the joining process. With a small house, plant a small tree. However, this principle can be altered. Use a large tree with a small house and you will make the house seem charming.

Proportion: Harmony of Parts to the Whole—Proportion is the harmonious relationship of one part to another and to the whole. A large paved terrace and a small lawn can be in proportion; on another site the patio can be small and the lawn large. To make both areas the same size is a mistake because one element does not complement the other. Visual appeal is lost because the eye regards both areas separately, not as a unit. Balance vertical forms with several horizontal elements.

Unity: Relationship of Materials to the Whole—Unity in a composition is the putting together of materials so that they become whole. You do not want a hodgepodge of unrelated masses insulting the eye. Well chosen plants of related forms, colors and textures achieve the unity every attractive garden needs.

Rhythm: Repetition of Elements—Another element to consider is rhythm in the composition. This involves repeating the same group of plants to give a sense of movement and balance—having elements of similar size, form and emphasis for use as one feature.

If you study each term individually, you will see that one depends on the other and that they are all interrelated. Generally, if you get the scale and proportion right, the other elements fall into line.

MAKING IT

No matter where the garden is located, to get the most out of the least space you will have to do some construction. One of the premises of small space gardening is to make full use of the vertical space—air space—which is neglected in most gardens. All kinds of post gardens, planter boxes, and trellis gardens can be built. This does not necessarily involve elaborate construction and these units give a garden character and dimension. In the following chapters you will find drawings, plans and directions for getting the most out of your small space.

Upper Photo
Repeating elements is pleasing to the eye. Small elements brought together can have a large impact.

Lower Photo
You can add planting area to your small space with simple construction, like the boxes in this steep backyard.

Opposite Page
A small garden can be both a place to sit and a scene to look at from your home inside.

SMALL GARDEN FOR RECTANGULAR LOT

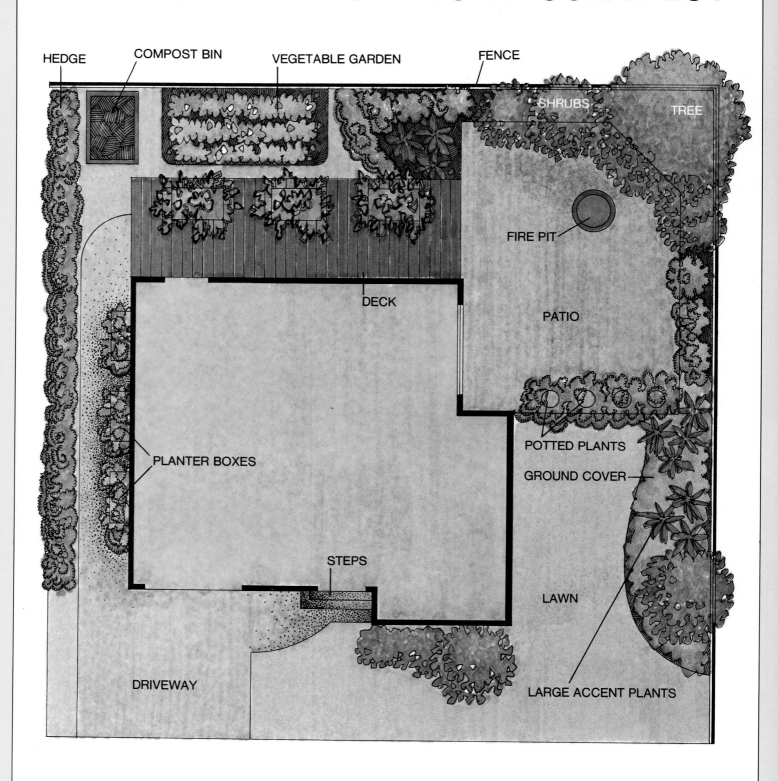

HEDGE

COMPOST BIN

VEGETABLE GARDEN

FENCE

SHRUBS

TREE

FIRE PIT

DECK

PATIO

PLANTER BOXES

POTTED PLANTS

GROUND COVER

STEPS

LAWN

DRIVEWAY

LARGE ACCENT PLANTS

SMALL GARDEN FOR LONG NARROW LOT

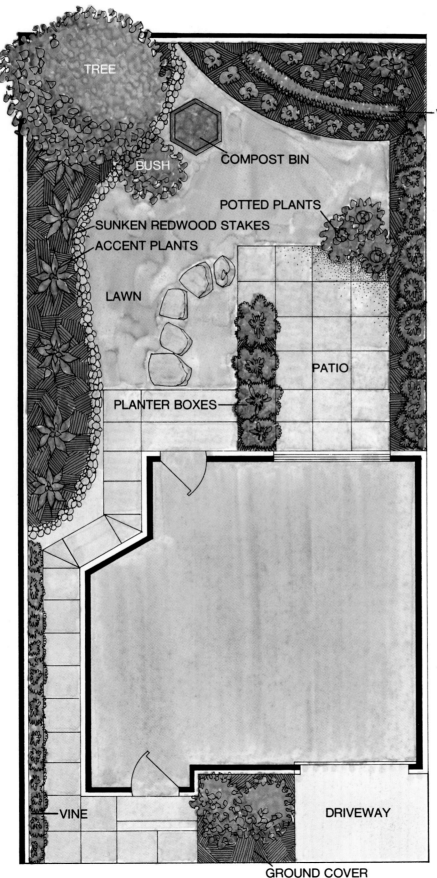

TREE

VEGETABLE GARDEN

COMPOST BIN

BUSH

POTTED PLANTS

SUNKEN REDWOOD STAKES

ACCENT PLANTS

LAWN

PATIO

PLANTER BOXES

VINE

DRIVEWAY

GROUND COVER

SMALL GARDEN FOR CORNER LOT

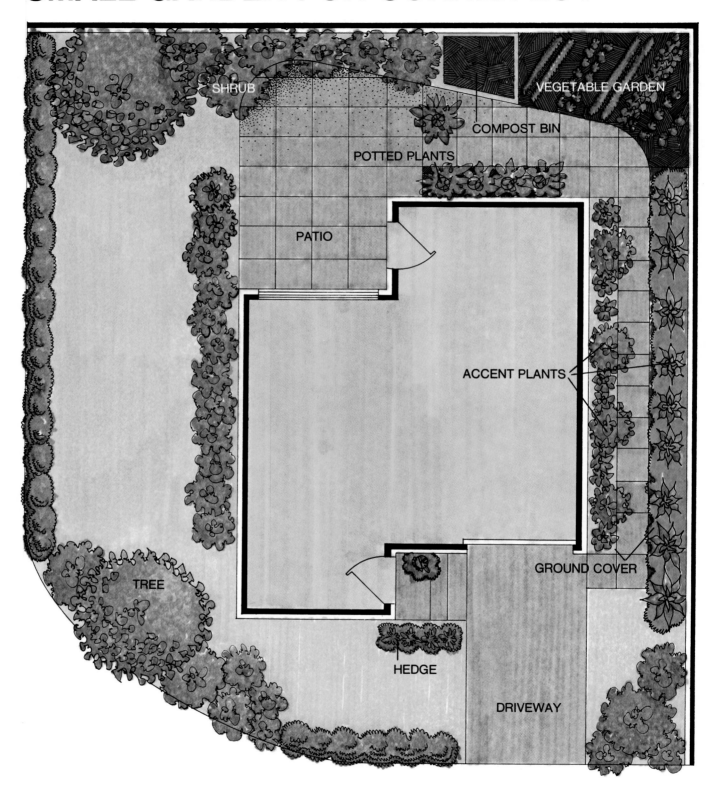

SHRUB

VEGETABLE GARDEN

COMPOST BIN

POTTED PLANTS

PATIO

ACCENT PLANTS

GROUND COVER

TREE

HEDGE

DRIVEWAY

SMALL GARDEN FOR WEDGE OR PIE-SHAPED LOT

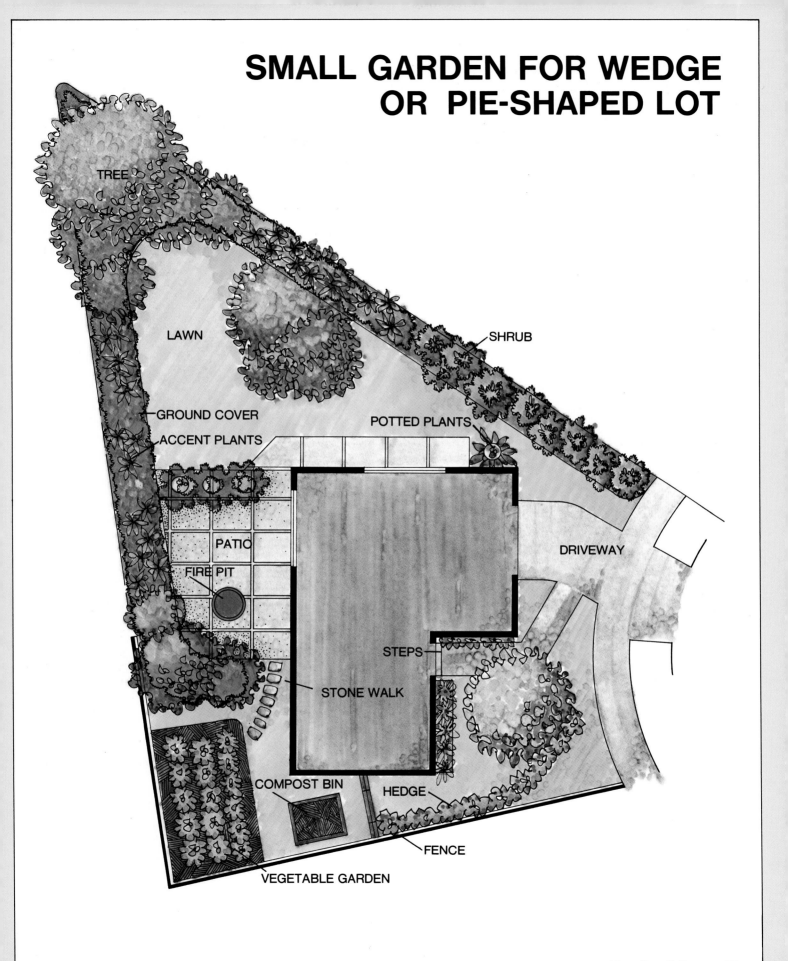

TREE

SHRUB

LAWN

GROUND COVER

POTTED PLANTS

ACCENT PLANTS

DRIVEWAY

PATIO

FIRE PIT

STEPS

STONE WALK

COMPOST BIN

HEDGE

FENCE

VEGETABLE GARDEN

Entrances, Atriums,
2 Sideyards & Backyards

Opposite page
An entrance garden should be inviting. It's here that your guests get their first impression of your home. A feeling of lushness and depth can be achieved by combining several different sized plants to create a vertical wall like this one. Photo by Roger Scharmer.

Below
Rocks define these small areas for planting colorful annuals.

Here we look at gardens at ground level—an entrance or atrium, sideyard or backyard. If you are considering a balcony, porch or rooftop garden, turn to chapter 3.

An entrance garden of, say, 10 by 15 feet is ample to create a beautiful scene—a welcome sight for guests.

The atrium garden is in the center of the home. It is basically an open court where you can grow many plants. Its chief benefit is as a scenic garden you can see from most rooms of the home. These small gardens, some no larger than 10 by 10 feet, can be almost priceless visual treasures. The backyard or sideyard greenery can be a handsome retreat.

Whether you have an entrance, atrium, backyard or sideyard garden, small though it may be, it can still be made to appear large. It's simply a matter of using available space. There will be more in-ground planting than plants in containers.

The care of ground gardens is somewhat different than container gardens. Plants in containers basically need more water because their roots are confined. Plants in

the ground spread their roots to seek water. We discuss some general care for ground gardens at the end of this chapter. Suggested plants for these areas are listed in Chapter 9.

ENTRANCE GARDENS

In some situations the house is set back from the street and this creates empty space in front of the house. Usually the area is not large, but it can afford a place for a garden. The problem in this situation is that the garden is exposed to all passers-by. Sometimes a wall can be built to create an courtyard-entry garden, but this is expensive. Usually, shrubs are used as barriers to give definition.

The plan of the entrance garden must be made with care; many times gardens grown strictly for display simply do not work well. It is hard to keep plants in prime condition all the time and, because this is where guests get their first impressions of the house, you will want your small space garden to look just right. A good solution, and one most frequently used, is to

ENTRANCE GARDEN

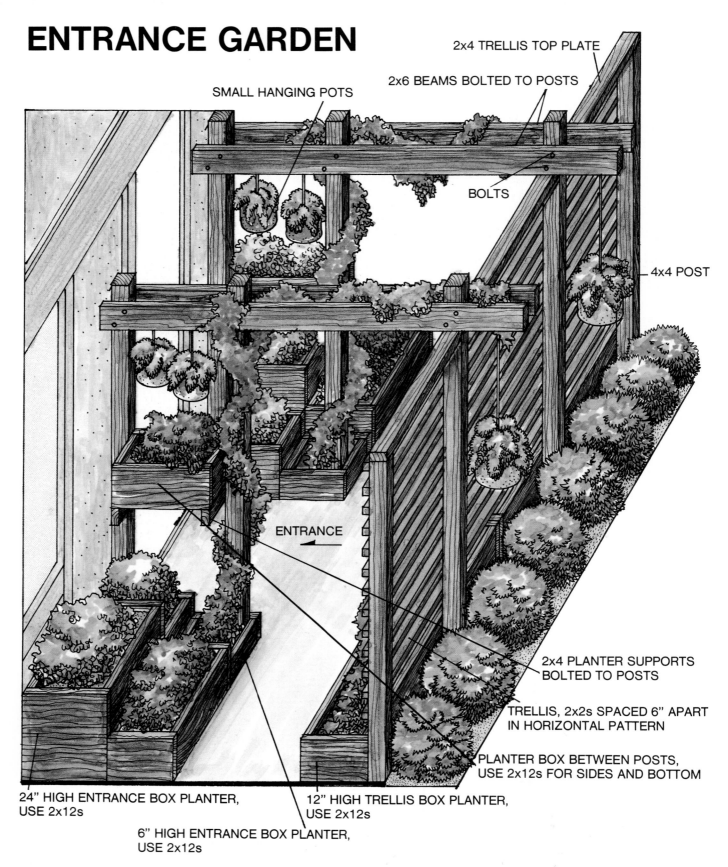

SMALL HANGING POTS

2x4 TRELLIS TOP PLATE

2x6 BEAMS BOLTED TO POSTS

BOLTS

4x4 POST

ENTRANCE

2x4 PLANTER SUPPORTS BOLTED TO POSTS

TRELLIS, 2x2s SPACED 6" APART IN HORIZONTAL PATTERN

PLANTER BOX BETWEEN POSTS, USE 2x12s FOR SIDES AND BOTTOM

24" HIGH ENTRANCE BOX PLANTER, USE 2x12s

12" HIGH TRELLIS BOX PLANTER, USE 2x12s

6" HIGH ENTRANCE BOX PLANTER, USE 2x12s

CONSTRUCTION DETAILS

ENTRANCE GARDEN

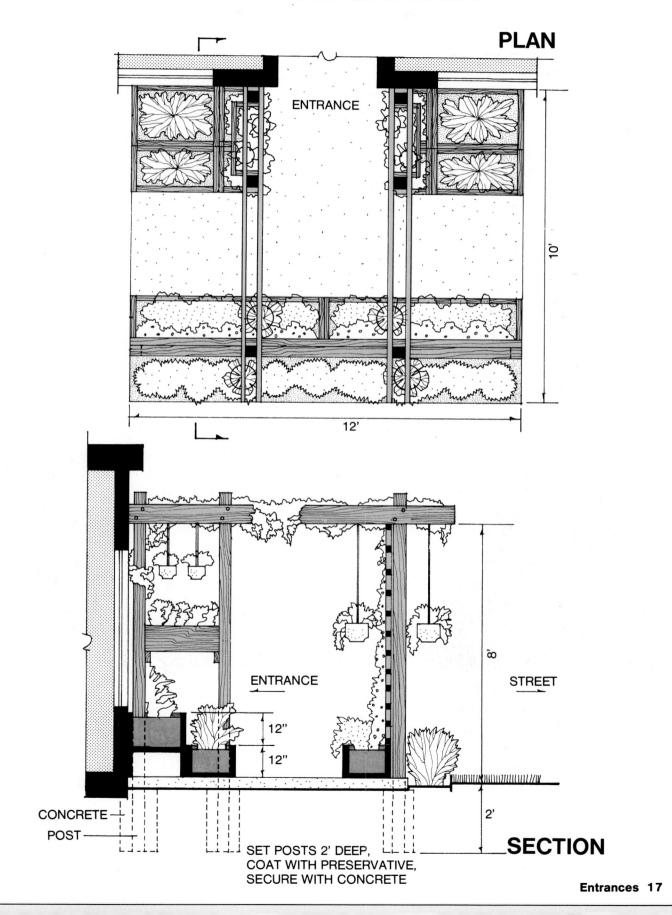

PLAN

ENTRANCE

10'

12'

SECTION

ENTRANCE

STREET

8'

12"

12"

2'

CONCRETE

POST

SET POSTS 2' DEEP,
COAT WITH PRESERVATIVE,
SECURE WITH CONCRETE

maintain a small lawn area and then concentrate areas of color around it. These borders of plants also are called *drifts*. Hedges and trees can be used to define the property.

How to Plant Drifts—Annuals and perennials work best. Select plants you like and place them in groups of 5 to 10 of the same species planted fairly close together. Add more plants if you have space. Always use three to five areas of color that complement each other. A single drift of plants looks like an isolated attempt at flower gardening left unfinished. Several drifts or areas of color create a balance and proportion.

The areas of flowers should be close to the house or far away, near the street side, but never in the center. Flowers situated midway on the property they will create a sawed-in-half look that is not appealing. Balance is the key word here. Plants are preferred either at the rear or front with the lawn as a carpet of green to create a unified look. Of course, the trees and shrubs serve as vertical accents.

As for walled entrance gardens, pretty though they are, they create a closed-in feeling that many people

object to. They can also be quite expensive to build. Think twice before you install a walled garden; it is not for everyone.

ATRIUM GARDENS

The atrium garden is surrounded by walls or windows of the home and it is a good solution in cities where you want privacy. Good layout is the secret to an attractive atrium garden. Because of its position, plants will always be on display, so careful planning is necessary. Use plants that look good and require low maintenance.

For a successful atrium garden, use the walls of the interior court for

Upper Photo
The formal look of this entrance garden matches the Colonial style of the house.

Lower Photo
This entrance garden conceals and softens the front of this house.

Opposite Page
This entrance garden is neither ostentatious or garish. A massive planting of one flower creates a dramatic scene. Photo by Jerry Bagger.

ATRIUM GARDEN

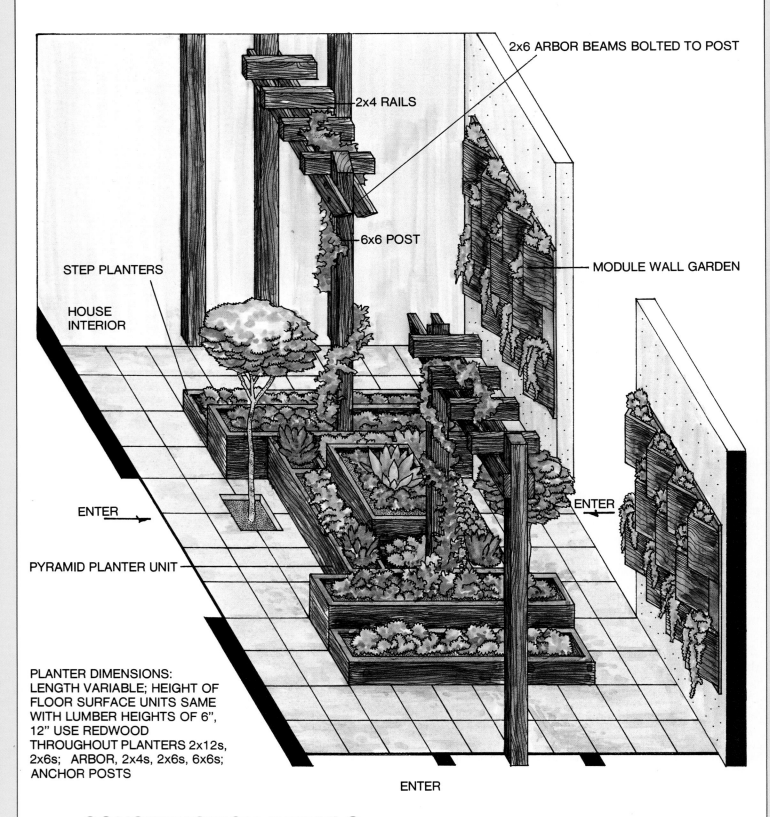

2x6 ARBOR BEAMS BOLTED TO POST

2x4 RAILS

6x6 POST

MODULE WALL GARDEN

STEP PLANTERS

HOUSE INTERIOR

ENTER →

PYRAMID PLANTER UNIT

ENTER

ENTER

PLANTER DIMENSIONS:
LENGTH VARIABLE; HEIGHT OF
FLOOR SURFACE UNITS SAME
WITH LUMBER HEIGHTS OF 6",
12" USE REDWOOD
THROUGHOUT PLANTERS 2x12s,
2x6s; ARBOR, 2x4s, 2x6s, 6x6s;
ANCHOR POSTS

CONSTRUCTION DETAILS

ATRIUM GARDEN

PLAN

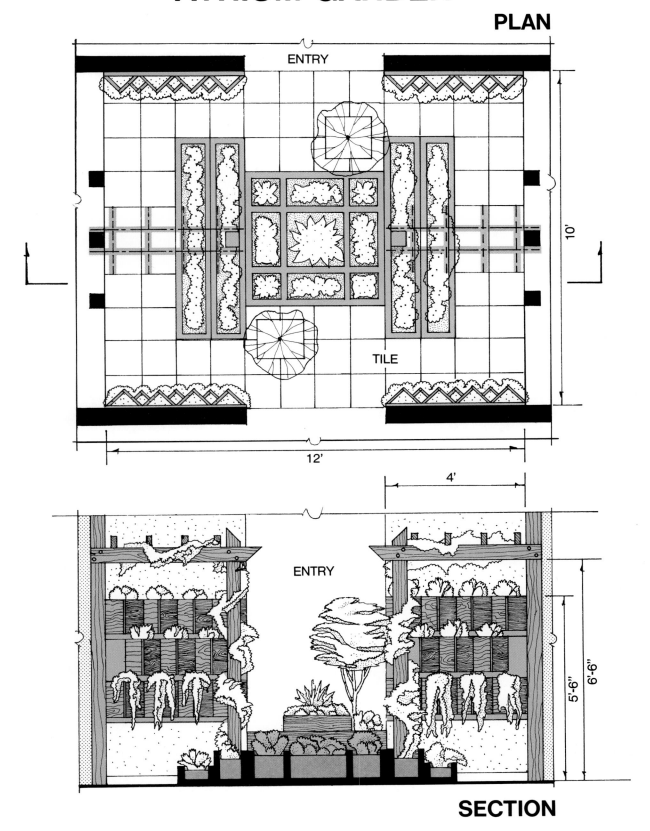

ENTRY

TILE

10'

12'

4'

ENTRY

5'-6"

6'-6"

SECTION

trelliswork. This will help eliminate the bare look that sometimes occurs. Select plants as if they were pieces of furniture; this is the place for lovely roses in containers, perhaps some fuchsias and dramatic specimen plants. Some small trees and graceful shrubs will complete the scene.

Unlike an entrance garden, in an atrium plan you can put flower beds in the center and leave paths around them. Or you can spot drifts of plants in one corner, having three or four drifts in one area. Balance this scene with a few container plants in other corners. Always leave room for access to the home and plenty of space for paths to get around the garden.

The atrium garden is generally an open, airy spot. It is more a Japanese-style arrangement where plants are sparse and the statement is made by the unused or *negative* area. A crowded garden can be attractive, but be sure to allow space for *you* and your activities.

Upper Photos
Enclosed or open, atriums add graceful beauty to any home.

Lower Photo
First impressions can make a visit a pleasure. Imagine the impact this wall of azaleas makes.

This entrance combines hanging containers and planting in the ground.

The surface of the atrium garden is very important, so be sure to make selections carefully. There are several alternatives. For example, you can grow a lawn or put in ground cover, with suitable paths of gravel. This works well and looks good. Other possibilities are patio-type floors or hard surfacing, but I find these areas less appealing than lawn or ground covers. You can also use loose fill materials like pea gravel or small-grade fir bark as a covering.

SIDEYARD GARDENS

If it is true that every problem is simply an opportunity in disguise, then sideyard gardens present a great opportunity to many small space gardeners. This neglected space, usually quite narrow, often dark, uncluttered and unattended, can add immeasurable beauty to the average home if it is properly utilized.

At the outset of this book I pointed out that it takes very little space to create a adequate garden. That is true even if the width of the space is very narrow. The average home and some condominiums have a surprising amount of usable foot-age running along both sides.

If your sideyard fits the dimensions of a balcony, and adequate sunlight is available, then our section on balcony gardening on page 37 can easily be adapted to your needs. However, if either or both of your sideyards are in shade, as is often the case in urban develop-

ments, your choice should be shade-tolerant plants. These may give a predominately green effect, but this doesn't mean drabness.

Green is an often overlooked or even mis-used color. Its full potential is rarely realized. Many gardeners consider green plants useful almost solely for backdrop, but in a sideyard they can provide a colorful study in hue and texture. Evergreens and shrubs are the obvious choices for narrow spaces because they require little maintenance. Green plants come in a variety of *shades* of green. There are shades of yellow, of blue and lush dark green and others in between. You can add

Upper Photo
The beauty of this sideyard clematis vine can be easily seen through the windows of the house, while the untidy lower portion remains hidden.

Lower Photo
This sideyard serves as a passageway from the front to the back of the house. Photo by Morley Baer.

Opposite Page
Privacy and quiet are characteristics of this small space garden. The sound of the recirculating fountain adds to the serenity and drowns out extraneous noises.

SIDEYARD GARDEN

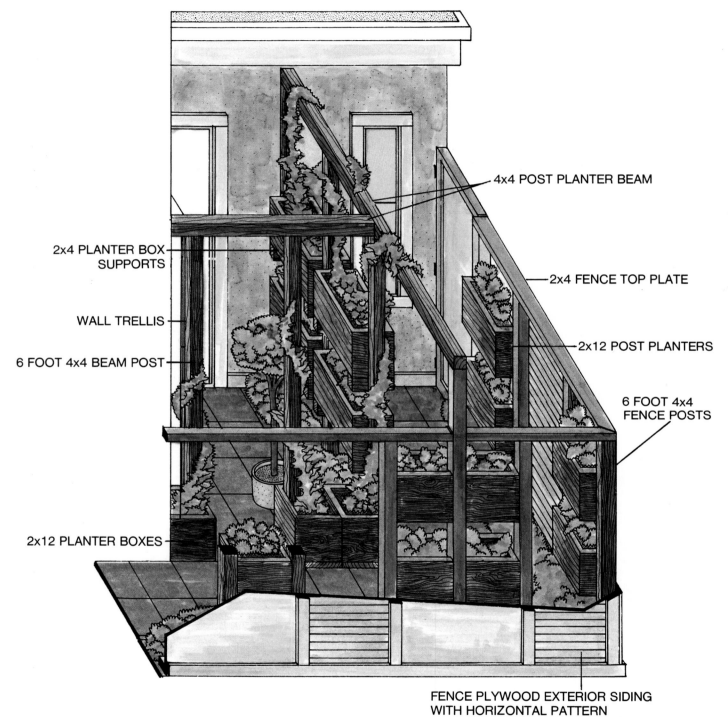

4x4 POST PLANTER BEAM

2x4 PLANTER BOX SUPPORTS

2x4 FENCE TOP PLATE

WALL TRELLIS

2x12 POST PLANTERS

6 FOOT 4x4 BEAM POST

6 FOOT 4x4 FENCE POSTS

2x12 PLANTER BOXES

FENCE PLYWOOD EXTERIOR SIDING WITH HORIZONTAL PATTERN

CONSTRUCTION DETAILS

SIDEYARD GARDEN

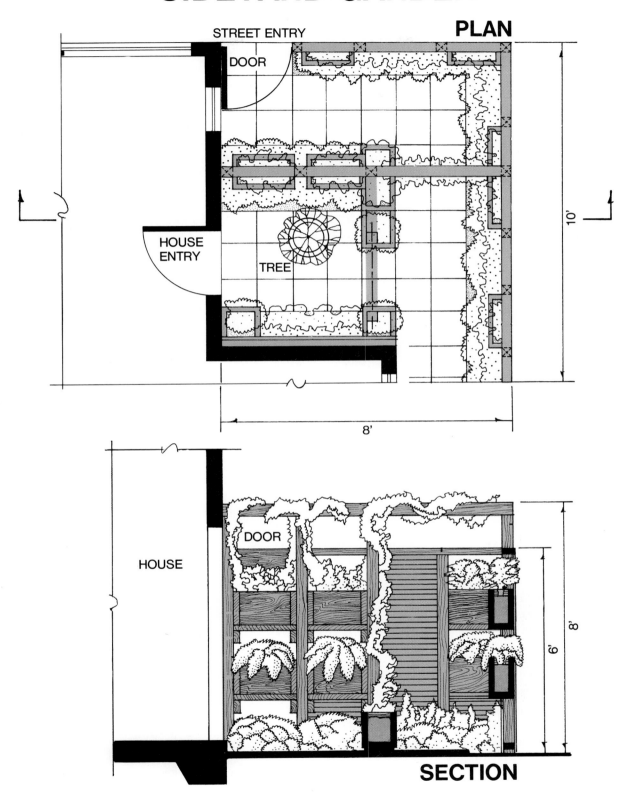

PLAN

STREET ENTRY

DOOR

HOUSE
ENTRY

TREE

10'

8'

HOUSE

DOOR

8'

6'

SECTION

A narrow lot in the city can be sterile and ugly, or it can be transformed into an inviting garden. Photo by Pat Matsumoto.

Upper Right
Juniper and jade plants set on a bed of volcanic rock make a neat low maintenance backyard.

Lower Right
Terracing gives good dimension and visual interest throughout this small area.

contrast by growing plants with rough bark alongside those with smooth bark. You can add visual appeal by growing plants with satin-textured leaves coupled with plants bearing rough dark-green velvet leaves. Or spindle-shaped leaves with broad ones—the number of possible combinations is huge.

Two things you should consider when planning your sideyard garden are the view from inside the house and the amount of sunlight coming in from the outside. Tall, narrow shrubs or vines on a trellis planted close to a window may look very handsome from the inside, but they can also decrease the amount of sunlight entering a room, making it gloomy. Plan for both the view and the sun by varying the height of the planting.

BACKYARD GARDENS

The backyard site is generally small and often narrow. These are the limitations but it is easy to work within them. A simple but cohesive design will create the most happy expression of plants and land. To achieve a measure of success, the garden must be an extension of the house, almost like another room although it is outside.

While the atrium or entrance gardens are usually limiting in what you can grow, the backyard offers enough space for all kinds of

Upper Photo
The mix of plants make this garden attractive.

Lower Photo
This backyard is small, but requires attention. The mums are replaced with new flowers each season.

gardens. A cutting garden along one side works well. Or a vegetable garden and special rose garden, for example, can be accommodated in the backyard site. While planning is important, it is not paramount as long as you stay within the realm of good design. Remember: scale, proportion and unity.

To achieve the big three, always *repeat plant material;* that is, if you have a clump of perennials at one corner, put in two more clumps nearby to balance the scene. Repetition of plant material is the key to the basic elements of design. But too much repetition, as in all things,

can ruin the results.

Generally, trees and shrubs will already be growing on the property. If they are not, you will have to put them in because a few good specimens of trees and shrubs form the backbone of any garden. These are the vertical accents and not many are needed—a few trees and perhaps a half dozen good shrubs will do the job admirably. Then you can select your flower garden, if you want one, and install a lawn or a vegetable site. The possibilities in the backyard garden are limitless; what you select depends on what pleases you.

Above
A garden of boxes and terracing in a 15-foot area creates a haven of color and beauty.

Opposite Page
This terrace provides four beds for a colorful cutting garden. The used bricks in the path are purposely set at random to give a more rustic feel.

Rooftops Balconies, Patios, & Porches

3

Opposite Page
This high balcony is ideal for sun-loving roses. The plants are arranged so they do not block the view. Photo by Jerry Bagger.

Upper Right
A productive vegetable garden only requires a few feet of space.

If you live in an apartment, flat, or townhouse, look upward and outward to the roof, porch, balcony or patio. There may be gardening spaces in all of these areas; but, to get the most out of your space, you should garden in containers or on supports. Balconies and roofs require creative planning. For instance, balconies usually are quite small, so you have to be imaginative. Roofs have to be strong enough to support the weight of plants and their containers. But again, these areas *can* and *should* be used for gardening—*everyone*, not just those who live in houses, has the right to enjoy the outdoors.

ROOF GARDENS

Before you start your roof garden, consider such questions as whether the roof will support the weight of

soil and planters. Are there drainage facilities for excess water? Is there a nearby water outlet? Will wind and sun or too much shade be a problem? Is the flooring suitable?

Most roofs can take the extra weight of a garden, but you cannot estimate how much weight any one roof will hold. It is essential to check with your building superintendent or your local city building and planning department. If the roof has to be strengthened, remember that a rooftop garden is economical because it increases the property value. Repair cracks or leaks and put up fences and railings for safety.

Rooftop gardens depend on planters and boxes to make them interesting and there are an infinite number of arrangements using containers. The main consideration with any small rooftop garden, or

ROOFTOP GARDEN

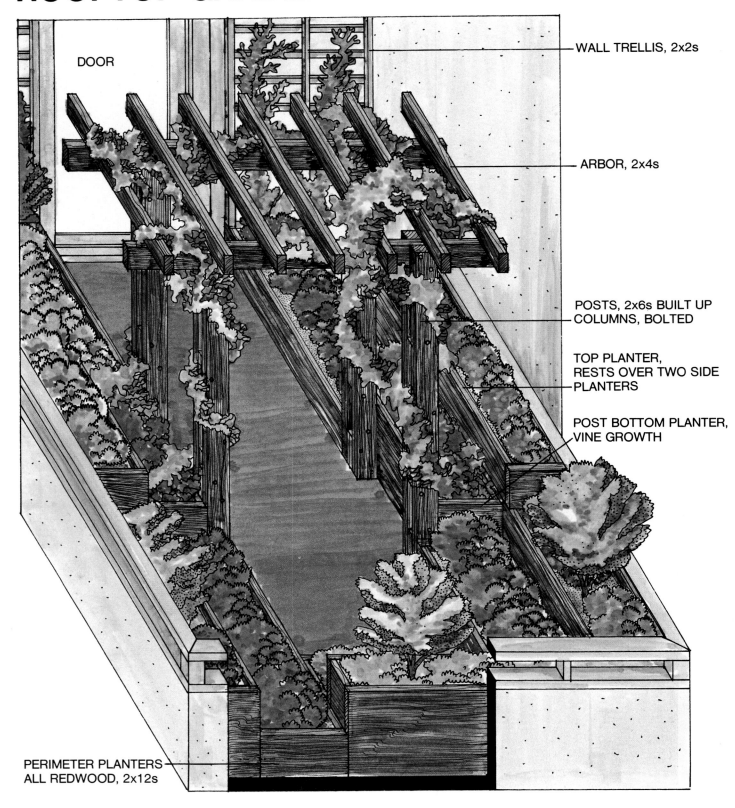

DOOR

WALL TRELLIS, 2x2s

ARBOR, 2x4s

POSTS, 2x6s BUILT UP
COLUMNS, BOLTED

TOP PLANTER,
RESTS OVER TWO SIDE
PLANTERS

POST BOTTOM PLANTER,
VINE GROWTH

PERIMETER PLANTERS
ALL REDWOOD, 2x12s

CONSTRUCTION DETAILS

ROOFTOP GARDEN

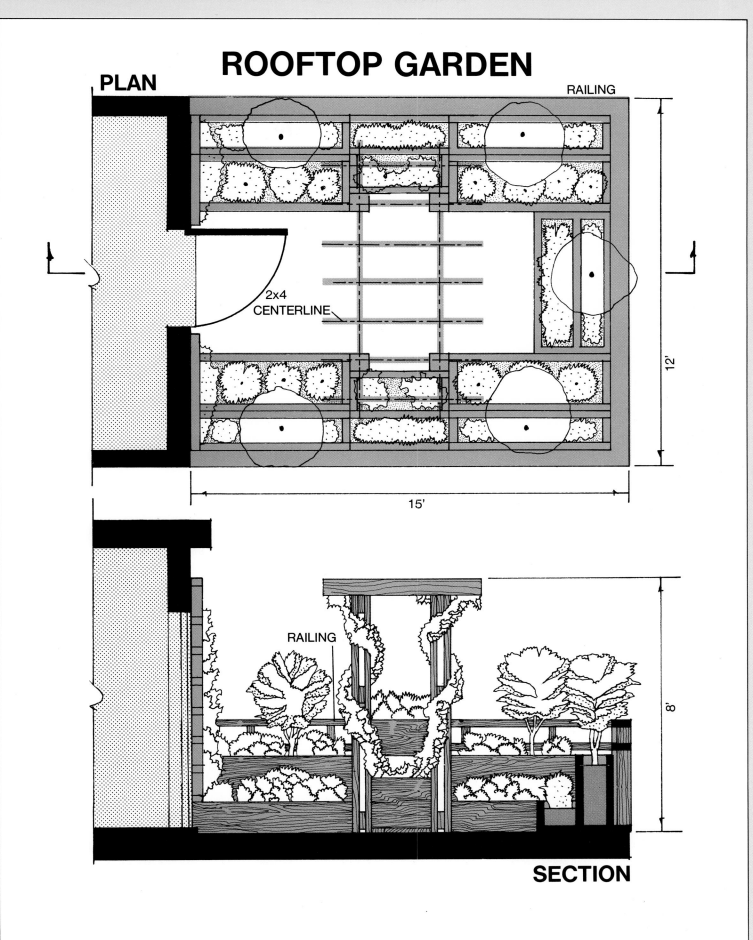

PLAN

RAILING

2x4
CENTERLINE

12'

15'

RAILING

8'

SECTION

Upper
A trellis overhead gives this small space area dimension and makes it seem like an outdoor room.

Lower Left
A small arbor, some shelves and a few planter boxes transformed this bare rooftop into an attractive greenery.

Lower Right
Some careful planning and a little construction organized this small roof to get the most out of its limited space.

any garden for that matter, is to leave enough space for walking or a chair and table where you can relax. A lush collection of your favorite foliage, color or vegetable plants makes a most inviting retreat.

BALCONIES AND PATIOS

Balconies can easily become indoor-outdoor gardens because they are accessible from inside. Unfortunately, they are often awkward in size, but you can overcome that problem. Wind will always be a problem, as will light if there is a balcony above you, so you must select plants carefully. And don't forget that with a balcony you may have to *carry* water to your plants. The particular problems of narrow balconies are discussed on page 68.

A patio usually is larger than a balcony so you can create a very fine small garden in this area, but it takes some planning. With patios it is best to concentrate your garden in one area and leave the remaining space for chairs or walking.

Planning your balcony or patio garden should begin with a sketch to give you the shape and size as a starting point to work from. Then start drawing in shapes of planters, pots and tubs. Try to balance the mass, line, and vertical and horizontal accents in the plan as shown in the drawings on the next pages.

The long and narrow balcony is the most common type in high-rise apartments. To add more growing space, place trellises at each end of the balcony. They will support

Upper
Pots and boxes were used to fill this 10- by 15-foot space.

Lower Left
You don't have to crowd your balcony with plants. A few properly placed specimens will do the job.

Lower Right
Planters placed along the edge of this roof provide space for seasonal plants.

BALCONY GARDEN

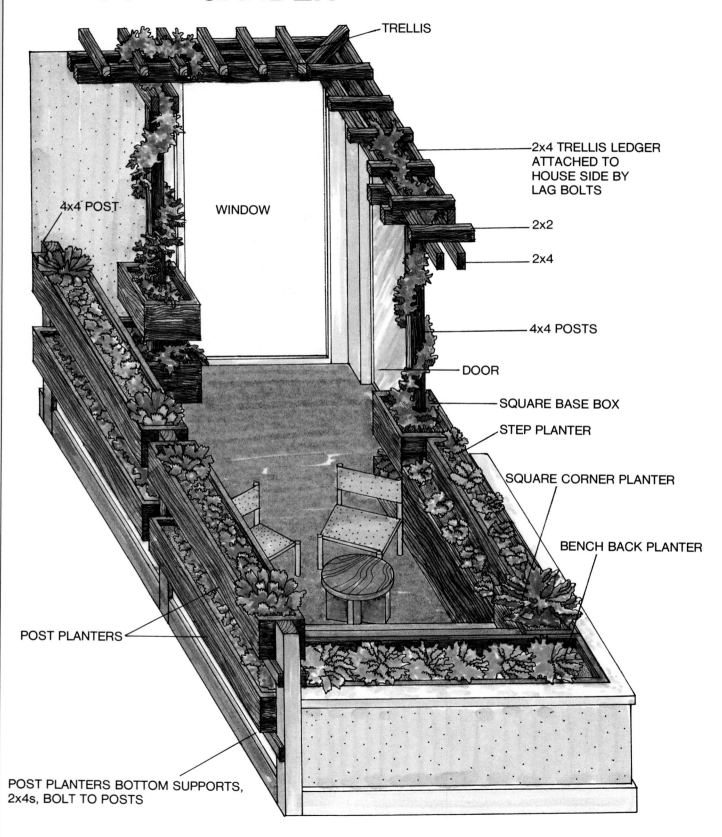

TRELLIS

2x4 TRELLIS LEDGER ATTACHED TO HOUSE SIDE BY LAG BOLTS

2x2

2x4

4x4 POST

WINDOW

4x4 POSTS

DOOR

SQUARE BASE BOX

STEP PLANTER

SQUARE CORNER PLANTER

BENCH BACK PLANTER

POST PLANTERS

POST PLANTERS BOTTOM SUPPORTS, 2x4s, BOLT TO POSTS

CONSTRUCTION DETAILS

BALCONY GARDEN

PLAN

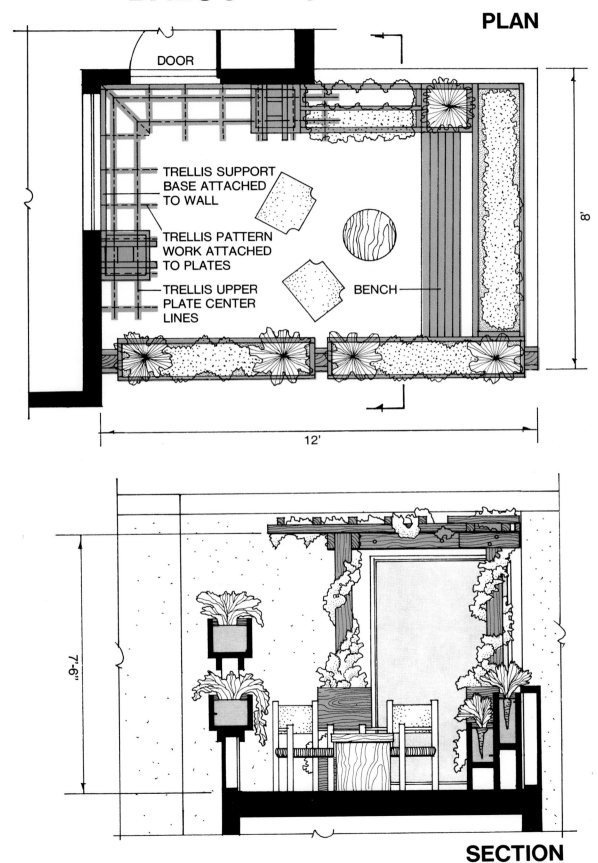

DOOR

TRELLIS SUPPORT
BASE ATTACHED
TO WALL

TRELLIS PATTERN
WORK ATTACHED
TO PLATES

TRELLIS UPPER
PLATE CENTER
LINES

BENCH

8'

12'

7'-6"

SECTION

plants and buffer the wind. Use the balcony ledge for pots; if the ledge is narrow, extend it with a wooden platform. Put a railing on the ledge for safety so pots won't be knocked off accidently. Other pots can go on platforms in groups. Several plants at different heights add dimension and scale to the small balcony. Use vining plants on the sides of the trellises and trailers on the ledges.

Make sure no one is under your balcony when you water your plants. Use large watering cans, especially if you are growing food plants, because they need lots of water as discussed in Chapter 8. You can use screening on the balcony. If you do, use narrow panels so you do not shut off the view. Use the screening only on one end; leave the other end open. To unite indoors with outdoors, set a pair of large plants indoors on each side of the entrance to the balcony. You'll be pleasantly surprised at the effect.

It is difficult to make a square patio or balcony look interesting. The secret is to create a center of interest. Use round tubs at one end to bring circles into the square design. Use several tubs of different heights, but of the same motif, in a corner to make a mass of green. In another corner put one attractive large plant in an ornamental pot to balance the scene. Hang some plants from the patio fence if there is one. Now bring the garden together with low masses of plants stretching from one area to another. This arrangement can be small pots in a row, or, even better, you can use a large planter filled with low-growing shrubs. Also, a trellis at one end of the patio will add vertical dimension.

Green, waterproof, indoor/outdoor carpeting on the patio will add interest and comfort and keep the place neater looking.

DECKS

The deck attached to your house makes an almost ideal site for your small space garden. Certainly it can enhance your home in a colorful fashion. As a matter of fact, it should bring out the artist in you because so many attractive designs are possible with your plants. If you do not have a deck it is relatively simple and inexpensive to add. By relatively simple I mean the construction of a fairly typical low-level deck on flat ground. Anything much more complicated than that kind of installation may require the aid of a professional. But as a general rule the home handyman will have no problem creating extra outdoor living space where he can put his green thumb to work.

As in all construction, first plan the details of the deck. Then check out your plan with the local building commission. Don't make the common error of building without legal clearance with the idea that "They can't tear it down." They *can* make you tear it down, so do it right from the beginning.

Most people think only of wood when they think of deck coverings. Certainly wood is a beautiful material, inexpensive when compared to some other building materials, and it's easy to use. But other materials can be used, including fiberglass, tile, concrete and, increasingly, exterior carpeting.

After you decide the size of deck you want, your lumber dealer will help you select the correct building materials for the job. Numerous kinds of wood are available. Various charts at your building materials center will indicate strength of the wood and the maximum spans for each type and size. You should check on these materials before you do a final drawing of your deck plan. The kind of wood you choose will help you decide such things as the distance between spans, footing locations, joist spans and spacings, and beams. The wood species itself is the determining factor.

PATIOS

Unlike a deck, which usually is constructed of wood above ground, the earth itself forms the support for a patio floor. Patios are ideal for container gardening. If there is no patio at your home, you can build one at a reasonable cost if you are careful. There are many options in materials and methods of construction, so plan your patio in detail if you intend to build it yourself. As in all forms of construction, check out your plan with the local building department or zoning board before laying your patio floor.

Materials for a patio floor usually

Upper Left
The framing for pouring the concrete was laid directly on the bulldozed subsoil.

Upper Right
Concrete is poured into the forms and smoothed. Anchor bolts placed in the wet concrete will hold supports for the patio roof.

Lower
The remaining space was covered with a 4-inch layer of top soil to assure good growing conditions.

Opposite Page
A brick floor and a wooden deck that fits right into the brick pattern gives this patio a unique character. Photo by Ken Molino.

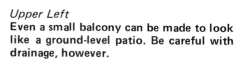

Upper Left
Even a small balcony can be made to look like a ground-level patio. Be careful with drainage, however.

Lower Left
Enclosing your patio in dense greenery gives a sense of privacy, but also a sense that the patio is part of a larger garden.

are concrete, stone, brick, flagstone, slate or tile. Other materials can be used as well.

Most patios are made of concrete because it is inexpensive and relatively easy to install. But most patio floors built of concrete are lifeless slabs of gray. They don't need to be. To add variety to your

patio it is possible to mix stains into the concrete for color, to expose the aggregate, to make patterns with a broom or trowel or even duplicate brick, stone or tile.

In planning your patio, remember the general coloring and texture of the house. Don't use materials that contrast garishly, but rather

A sideyard patio doesn't need much room. This one is only 5 feet wide.

Opposite Page, Upper Right
This tucked-in patio provides a pleasant, peaceful place to sit. Photo by Roger Scharmer.

Opposite Page, Lower Right
A patio off the house becomes an additional attractive living area.

use those that will blend harmoniously.

When the building material is concrete, codes sometimes specify steel mesh or gravel subbase or both. The intent of these regulations is to protect your concrete from cracking. But as a general rule, unless the law requires them, I wouldn't use either. Careful installation of quality materials will do more to prevent cracking than steel. A gravel subbase is necessary only to prevent *frost-heave* in soils that don't drain well. Water held by such soils expands as it freezes and can crack concrete.

Whether you're laying concrete,

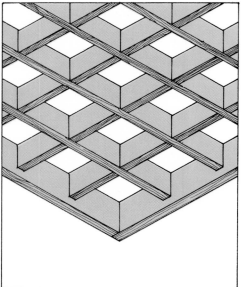

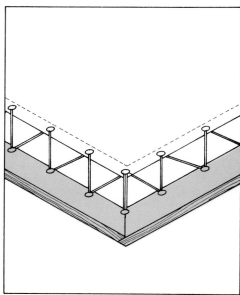

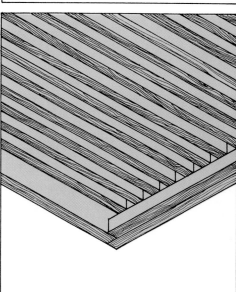

OVERHEAD SHADES

TOP LEFT, EGG CRATE
TOP RIGHT, STRUNG CANVAS
BOTTOM RIGHT, LOUVERED BOARDS

HINTS ON MATERIALS

● Try to design structures with lengths of rafters, beams and posts in *even* inches because this is the way lumber is sold.

● Use common-dimension lumber such as 2x4, 2x6, or 4x4, 4x6 and so on. Lumber yards usually do not consider other sizes as stock items and will charge more for them. Check page 89 for the actual dimensions of common lumber sizes.

● Keep your covering material in mind as you plan. Materials such as fiberglass come in stock sizes; plan for these dimensions.

● When purchasing lumber, specify the grade, quantity, type of wood, thickness, width and length, in that order.

bricks or other materials, remember to make sure water will drain away from any structures. Poor drainage can lead to larger problems and you may want to consult a professional. And, unless you're a skilled craftsman, don't choose a very complicated pattern when laying brick.

ROOFING IT

Either a deck or a patio can be covered with a roof. Rafters and beams carry the roof load to the posts, and rafter sizes are the easiest to determine. The *width* of the roof becomes the rafter length. Then the *center-to-center spacing* of the beams is figured. Beams run lengthwise and general rules for figuring beam size are: a 4-foot span requires a 4x4 inch beam; a 6-foot span requires a 4x6 inch beam; an 8-foot span requires a 4x8 inch beam. These are general dimensions for temperate climates. In areas where snow load is heavy, rafters and beams will have to be heavier.

Beams throw the weight load to the *posts*, which then carry it to the

foundation or building *piers.* The universal post is a 4x4. It supports a very heavy roof load and you are not likely to need a heavier post unless the patio is so large that a heavier post is more in proportion with the total structure.

For most patio overhangs or roofs, the wall of the house is used as a support and the point of connection is of vital importance. Generally, the overhead shelter is attached to the main house with a sloping roof and *eave* line. The patio roof can be attached to the roof, the wall or, in some cases, the eaves. You can determine the best way for your own personal situation. Check local building ordinances. Also, make sure you build the patio roof high enough so it clears the tops of all swinging doors and windows on the house.

Attaching the overhead structure to the house wall is the easiest and safest method of construction. If your eave line is high enough, you can set the rafters under the gutter and anchor directly into the house wall. The simplest way to do this is to fasten a long board to the house wall where rafters can rest. This *ledger* will carry the weight and should be anchored securely to the studs in the wall with lag screws or spikes. Otherwise the ledger is likely to give way. Studs are generally spaced 16 or 18 inches apart. Use a stud finder, available at hardware stores, to find the wall studs.

If the wall is textured or stuccoed, you will have to drill holes to attach screws or lag bolts. Use a masonry bit in a power drill. If the wall is concrete or brick, drill in at least 2 to 3 inches and then fit lead sleeves into the holes. Then bolt the ledger in place.

To anchor the rafters on the ledger, you can rest them on the wood and toenail them in place, or better yet use metal *joist holders*, available at lumber yards, which give a more solid support.

If you attach the overhead structure to the eaves or facing strip, be extremely careful. These are generally the weakest possible points for supporting additional weight. Use metal fastening strips to assure that the rafters stay in place. Where the fascia is thin stock, it is better to replace it with 2-inch stock.

If you decide to anchor the overhead directly to the roof, lay the ledger strip on the roof and attach it with lag bolts driven through the roof into the house rafters. Position the ledger strip above the wall of the house to distribute the extra weight evenly and reduce the strain on the roof. Then toenail the patio roof rafters to the ledger. Be sure to caulk this line so water doesn't leak through.

WOOD OVERHANGS

There are several inexpensive kinds of wood available to cover the framing once it is built.

Lath—This is outdoor rough-surfaced redwood or cedar 3/8 inch thick and 1-5/8 inches in width. It is usually sold in lengths of 2 or 8 feet in bundles of 50. Ask for *standard lathing lumber*.

Batten—Battens are larger than laths. They are milled to 3/4 inch thick in widths of 2 to 3 inches. They can be bought by the piece in lengths up to 20 feet. There are rough-surfaced battens and smooth battens.

Boards—Depending on your design, you can use 1x4, 2x2, 1x2 or 1x3 boards in thickness of 1-1/4 inches. Construction-grade lumber is satisfactory. If you want a more finished look, kiln-dried lumber can be used, but it will cost you at least 20 percent more.

PORCHES

Older homes and flats often have porches that can be turned into attractive gardens.

Most porches already have guard rails and wooden floors, so little alteration is involved. It is the arrangement of plants that is most important. Build boxes to fit specific areas so the porch garden has a handsome, custom-made look. Consider growing flowering vines to cover walls. Otherwise, grow the plants you want. In most areas, your flowering plants will thrive from April to September.

A porch may be U-shaped or L-shaped and a simple series of planter boxes along the edges below the railing will enhance its appearance. A better arrangement is to stack boxes or use a group of post gardens to create vertical greeneries while increasing your total space. Or you may prefer to have a corner garden using planters at various heights. In any case, our drawings will help you select a plan that will turn any small porch into a veritable jungle.

Below
This wooden deck is built on three levels, leading toward the house. This gives the impression of a larger space than is really there.

Opposite Page
A wooden deck built over old concrete created this elegant scene. Tulips and armeria (thrift) planted in boxes bloom profusely.

PORCH GARDEN

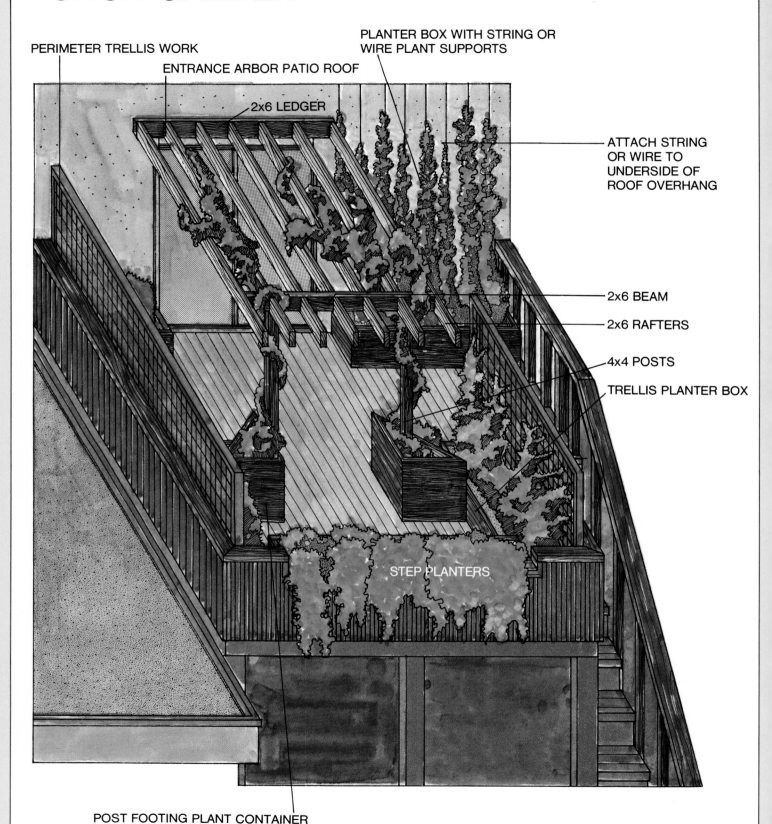

PERIMETER TRELLIS WORK

ENTRANCE ARBOR PATIO ROOF

PLANTER BOX WITH STRING OR WIRE PLANT SUPPORTS

2x6 LEDGER

ATTACH STRING OR WIRE TO UNDERSIDE OF ROOF OVERHANG

2x6 BEAM

2x6 RAFTERS

4x4 POSTS

TRELLIS PLANTER BOX

STEP PLANTERS

POST FOOTING PLANT CONTAINER

PORCH GARDEN

PLAN

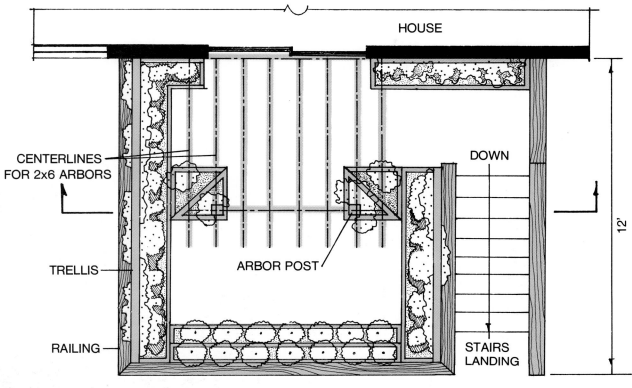

HOUSE

CENTERLINES
FOR 2x6 ARBORS

DOWN

TRELLIS

ARBOR POST

12'

RAILING

STAIRS
LANDING

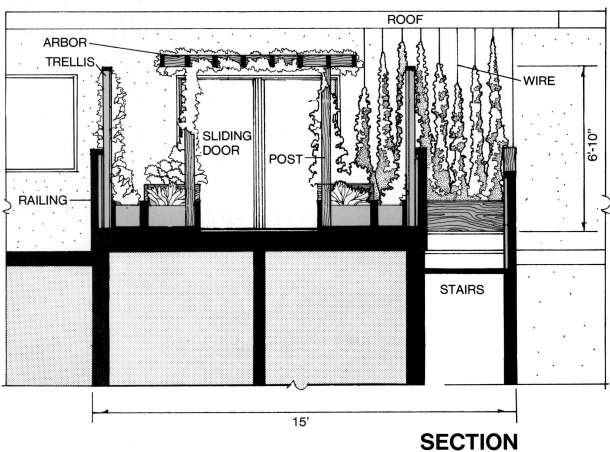

ROOF

ARBOR

TRELLIS

WIRE

SLIDING
DOOR

POST

RAILING

6'-10"

STAIRS

15'

SECTION

Terraced & City Gardens 4

Opposite
Terraces built with rocks give a natural effect. Armeria, sparaxis and lillies add color and shape.

TERRACED GARDENS

Stripped to its essentials, a *terrace* is nothing more than a raised, flat mound of earth with sloping sides. Or, more commonly, the terrace is thought of as a *series* of flat platforms of earth rising one above the other. Do not confuse the constructed *true* terrace with the level paved outdoor living area, many times called a terrace, which is generally an expansive patio.

The terraced garden, the kind we deal with, is a stair-step arrangement that requires more work to install, but once in place it is a great space-saver. Furthermore, plants at raised levels are easier to care for than plants in the ground because there is little or no squatting or stooping.

If your yard is on a hillside, the terrace garden is the only answer to sensible gardening. But even if your garden must be on a level area, terracing still makes sense. This kind of gardening requires careful planning, so approach it with your eyes wide open. In this chapter we will show you how to install a terrace garden so you can get several plants in a small place.

Some construction and *fill,* which is essentially rubble, are necessary to make this garden. But despite the extra effort, there are certain intangible benefits. Terraced gardens have an elegance and character that are always appealing.

CONSTRUCTION

Don't let the word scare you. Terracing means putting in some fill and building some wooden barriers to contain the soil. This is not difficult and can be done inexpensively. If your garden is on a hillside, construction is simple; on level land it requires more planning. Either way, it is possible to have a stair-step arrangement or a multi-level garden. For simplicity we call it a terraced garden. Basically, this is a raised garden bed. In levels of three, such

as I have in my own garden, they make unusally good space-saving gardens.

For the walls of the terraces, which are actually retaining walls, most people use wood. But masonry, which is expensive, or stone also can be used. I recently saw a stone terraced garden that was a knockout. Here, however, the owner had a great deal of time and liked to work with stone. For most people wood is less expensive and easier to work with.

My terraced garden was built with 2x12 boards fastened to 2x4 posts in a square or four-sided pattern. First, I dug holes about 28-inches deep for the posts and set these in concrete; then I waited for two days for the concrete to harden so the posts would be secure. Then I attached the boards to make the wooden boxes. These boxes do not need to be built with the same care as finished furniture. Eventually some vegetation will cover them so your mistakes will be well hidden. However, the containers must be *strong* to hold the weight of the soil. Drive several nails into them and be sure they are well fastened at the corners. Drawings in this chapter will help you make your terraced garden. The arrangement, however, can take several forms. Your garden need not be stair-stepped or tiered as shown. For example, it can be *modular*, that is, a standardized design that can be arranged or fitted together in a variety of ways. Or, the boxes can be placed at random in your yard.

PREPARING
THE TERRACED GARDEN

Painstaking care should be taken in preparing the soil for any garden. This one is no exception. Because you are filling huge boxes you can use *fill* at the base. Fill may be pieces of bricks or concrete or almost any type of debris that is worked into

the existing soil. This creates the layer or *bed* for the topsoil. Once the fill is in place, the bed should be covered with 18 to 20 inches of good topsoil. Leave at least 2 to 3 inches between the top of the soil and the top of the boards. Rake and pulverize the soil so it is porous.

RETAINING WALLS

Retaining walls do more than hold back a mound of dirt. They can and should be decorative, too. A so-called dry stone wall installation with plants in earth "pockets" is quite effective in the garden. Cascading plants such as sedums and ice plants covering the sharp edges of masonry or wooden retaining walls can be quite attractive.

The dry wall method of installation is easy. There is no mortar used in this installation, hence the term "dry." The stones are used to hold back relatively low banks of earth. Leave pockets of earth between the stones. The stones should be positioned to pitch the wall back toward the thrust of the slope. As a general rule, they should be long and flat. The topmost stone should be placed several inches inwards from the last stone on the bottom.

Dry stone walls are not difficult

Sedums and other succulents placed against a fence and accented by white brick make a handsome garden.

Opposite Page, Upper Left
Terracing at the side of house was done by stacking two 2x12-inch redwood boards and attaching them to posts sunk in the ground.

Opposite Page, Upper Right
Letting the vegetation cover the terraces can create a handsome effect.

Opposite Page, Lower Left
A brick path and low terraces can be used as a stairway.

Opposite Page, Lower Right
This terrace climbs with the fence to create usable planting space.

to build and they offer the gardener a bonus: the chance to grow small plants between the stones. It is a fascinating kind of gardening, very decorative for a very small place. Dry walls should not exceed 4 feet. Higher walls are apt to tumble with time if there are severe rains. Check local zoning ordinances before constructing any walls.

A retaining wall more than 4 feet high is not easy to build. It is best to seek professional help for such structures. A wall that is not properly engineered and built might collapse after the first few rain storms. However, low walls can be built easily and inexpensively by the average homeowner.

Be sure to plan for ample water drainage when building any retaining wall. Soil absorbs a large quantity of water during a rainy season;

TERRACED GARDEN

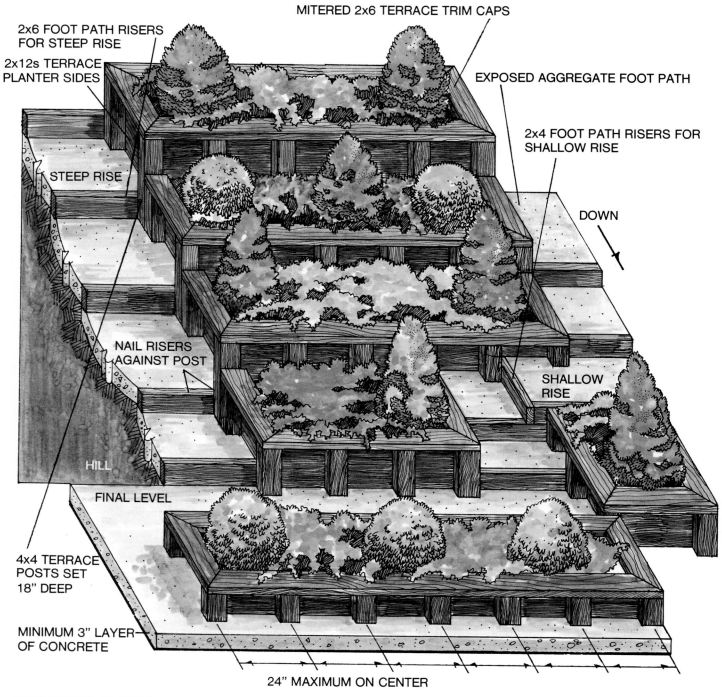

2x6 FOOT PATH RISERS
FOR STEEP RISE

2x12s TERRACE
PLANTER SIDES

MITERED 2x6 TERRACE TRIM CAPS

EXPOSED AGGREGATE FOOT PATH

2x4 FOOT PATH RISERS FOR
SHALLOW RISE

STEEP RISE

DOWN

NAIL RISERS
AGAINST POST

SHALLOW
RISE

HILL

FINAL LEVEL

4x4 TERRACE
POSTS SET
18" DEEP

MINIMUM 3" LAYER
OF CONCRETE

24" MAXIMUM ON CENTER

DIMENSIONS: PLANTER UNITS
VARIABLE; STEPS VARIABLE

LUMBER: 2x12s FOR ALL SIDES,
ALL REDWOOD OR TREATED
OTHER SPECIES

HARDWARE: GALVANIZED NAILS;
WIRE MESH IN CONCRETE; BOLT
POSTS TO SIDES IF DESIRED,
OTHERWISE NAIL

TERRACED GARDEN

LOW TERRACES ALONG A STEEP HILL MADE OF 4x4s AND 2x8 AND 2x10 REDWOOD ENSURES PROPER DRAINAGE. A SINGLE HIGH WALL IS LIKELY TO TOPPLE DUE TO INCREASED WATER PRESSURE AFTER A RAIN.

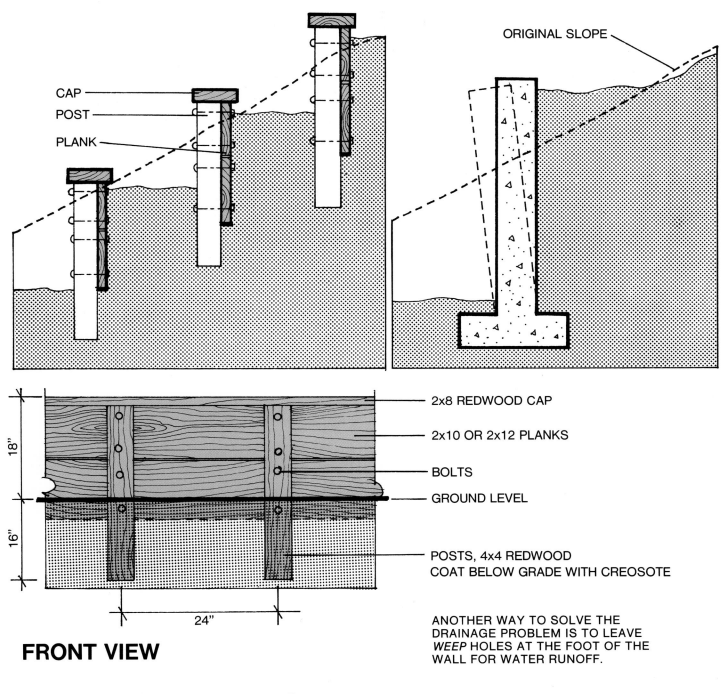

CAP
POST
PLANK

ORIGINAL SLOPE

2x8 REDWOOD CAP

2x10 OR 2x12 PLANKS

BOLTS

GROUND LEVEL

POSTS, 4x4 REDWOOD
COAT BELOW GRADE WITH CREOSOTE

18"

16"

24"

FRONT VIEW

CONSTRUCTION DETAILS

ANOTHER WAY TO SOLVE THE DRAINAGE PROBLEM IS TO LEAVE *WEEP* HOLES AT THE FOOT OF THE WALL FOR WATER RUNOFF.

it flows downhill below the surface. It accumulates where the water hits the wall, building up pressure, and it may burst the wall.

Leaving *weep holes* or gaps in the wall is the simplest way to drain away excess water. Tile and gravel backfill also prevents undermining of a low wall. However, for a higher wall you probably would need an additional reinforcing wall of masonry. Building codes often require extensive and expensive testing when large amounts of fill are planned.

Where weep holes are used, construct a special gutter to carry off water so it doesn't ruin a patio or lawn. Standard drain tiles or rounded concrete gutters can be used. All gutters should be wide enough to be easily cleaned. It may be necessary to shovel away debris such as leaves or twigs.

Remember this warning: Where the wall is taller than 4 feet or the slope of the hillside more than 30 percent, use professional help. Consult your local building code before you build anything.

MASONRY RETAINING WALLS

A masonry retaining wall may be brick, concrete block or cast concrete. In any event, it is better to have a series of low walls than one high one— it is less likely to lean or break under pressure. Concrete foundations and reinforcing rods will be necessary to construct any masonry wall.

Brick retaining walls are lovely, but they are difficult to build. Even when securely mortared they do not have the holding power of a concrete wall. Reinforcing rods are necessary in brick walls, as are weep holes, and building a brick wall is a job best left to the professional. However, for all their problems, a brick wall lends old-world charm to a garden. So if it is your choice, have it built, but be sure it is built to last.

WOODEN RETAINING WALLS

Redwood or cedar boards frequently are used for low retaining walls and terrace beds. They are handsome and function well if built properly. However, even with these resistant woods, use a fungicide preservative on any wooden member that comes into contact with the soil. If possible use *pressure-treated* wood. If you must apply the preservative yourself, a number are available. Check with a paint store.

Generally, 2 x 12-inch boards are run horizontally with 4 x 4-inch posts supporting them. Dig deep holes, about 28 inches, and use a gravel base as you would for regular fence work. Place posts every 4 feet for support. You might also want to brace the wall with wooden members.

Plant vines and trailers in the ground. In time they will drape the wall in rich green.

RECIPE FOR CONCRETE

Everyone has a favorite formula for concrete. So do I.

For walling footings and foundations I recommend that you use 6 gallons of water for each sack of cement. To mix the concrete, add 2 shovels of gravel and the same amount of sand to the cement and mix. Add water from a garden hose, a little at a time, mixing as you go. Continue mixing all ingredients until they are well combined and of the desired stiffness. If the mix is too watery, add some more sand, gravel and cement. If it is too thick, add more water. This recipe works whether you are mixing by hand or with a power mixer.

MAINTAINING A TERRACE

Caring for the terraced garden is perhaps more simple than gardening on level ground. By its very construction the terraced garden affords excellent drainage. Actually, water runs from one raised bed to another and on to the next, so

Opposite Page
A low terrace constructed with rock lifts the planting level to the top of the stairs. Brilliant white candytuft accents the terrace border. Photo by John Warner.

Upper Left
This is sometimes called a planter box, but is really terracing. Photo by Ken Molino.

Upper Right
This condo garden was kept simple to reduce maintenance.

Lower Left
This garden combines terraces with modular boxes of geraniums and azaleas. Modular units are discussed in the next chapter.

CITY TREES AND SHRUBS
Deciduous Trees
Acer palmatum (Japanese Maple)
Acer rubrum (Red Maple)
Albizia julibrissin (Silk Tree)
Betula populifolia (Gray Birch)
Carpinus betulus pyramidalis (Pyramidal hornbeam)
Cornus florida (Flowering Dogwood)
Ginkgo bilboba (Maidenhair Tree)
Koelreuteria paniculata (Golden-rain Tree)
Laburnum vossi (Goldenchain Tree)
Malus (Flowering Crab Apple)

Robinia (Locust)
Salix babylonica (Weeping Willow)
Sorbus aucuparia (European Mountain Ash)

Evergreen Trees
Picea abies or *excelsa* (Norway Spruce)
Pinus mugo (Mountain or Swiss Pine)
Pinus strobus (White Pine or Eastern White Pine)
Pinus sylvestris (Scots or Scotch Pine)
Taxus (Yew)

Shrubs
Abelia grandiflora (Glossy Abelia)
Chaenomeles japonica (Japanese Quince)
Cotoneaster (Cotoneaster)
Euonymus (Euonymus)
Forsythia (Forsythia)
Ilex (Holly)
Ligustrum (Privet)
Philadelphus (Mock Orange)
Pyracantha (Firethorn)
Rhododendron (Rhododendron, Azalea)
Rosa (Rose)
Salix discolor (Pussy Willow)

drainage is rarely a problem. Moisture that is not captured in the top tier goes into the second tier and so on.

General watering and feeding practices are the same for terraced gardens as for the gardens discussed in chapter 8. You will find lists of plants for your terraced gardens in Chapter 11. A special list of plants best suited for city gardens is included in this chapter.

CITY GARDENS

A garden in the city is, of course, highly desirable. It offers a welcome retreat from crowded places and provides that touch of green so lacking in most urban areas.

Plan your city garden carefully and make every inch of space count. You can do it by following the examples in this book. Create small islands of color; you don't need too many plants, but you need enough to create a total harmonious picture. Use a few small trees, some shrubs, drifts of annuals and perennials and seasonal plants in pots. Remember to leave space for walking so you can enjoy your garden. Do not use large trees or shrubs or those that have sprawling growth. Keep plant materials in scale as we discussed in Chapter 1.

CARE

Garden culture is basically the same for plants in the city as it is for any garden. Be sure you provide good porous soil. Feed plants moderately and protect them from insects and diseases. Water plants regularly, at least twice a week in spring and summer. Prune and trim trees and shrubs as necessary.

All gardens should be kept in top shape, but the city garden requires the most attention because it is always on display. See Chapter 8 for basic cultural rules. One good tip: Use as many vines as possible in the city. They cover walls and corners and can create a good frame for the garden.

CITY PLANTS

Some plants can withstand the rigors of city conditions better than others and, while you can plant almost anything in a city, the plants on the opposite page are highly recommended.

City gardens often mean balcony gardens like this one in New York. Read both this chapter and Chapter 5 if you have a balcony.

TYPICAL CITY GARDEN

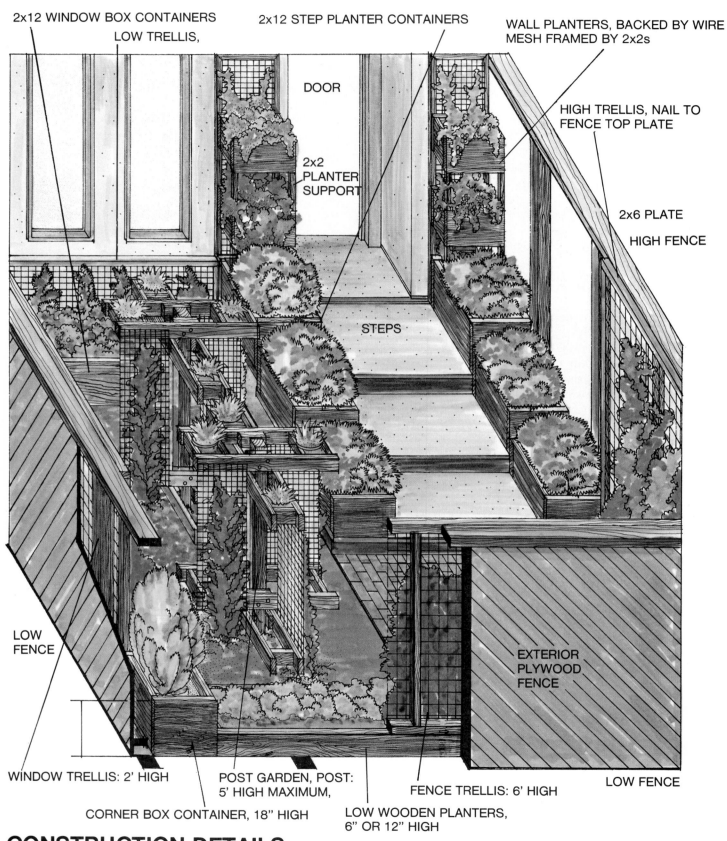

2x12 WINDOW BOX CONTAINERS

LOW TRELLIS,

2x12 STEP PLANTER CONTAINERS

WALL PLANTERS, BACKED BY WIRE MESH FRAMED BY 2x2s

DOOR

HIGH TRELLIS, NAIL TO FENCE TOP PLATE

2x2 PLANTER SUPPORT

2x6 PLATE

HIGH FENCE

STEPS

LOW FENCE

EXTERIOR PLYWOOD FENCE

WINDOW TRELLIS: 2' HIGH

POST GARDEN, POST: 5' HIGH MAXIMUM,

FENCE TRELLIS: 6' HIGH

LOW FENCE

CORNER BOX CONTAINER, 18" HIGH

LOW WOODEN PLANTERS, 6" OR 12" HIGH

CONSTRUCTION DETAILS

TYPICAL CITY GARDEN

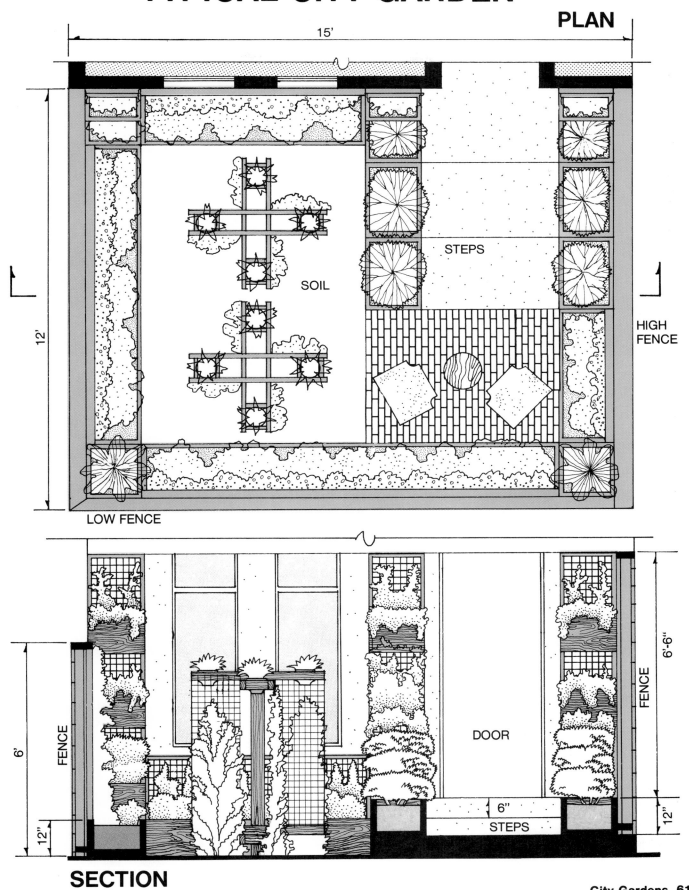

PLAN

15'

12'

STEPS

SOIL

HIGH FENCE

LOW FENCE

SECTION

FENCE

6'

12"

DOOR

6'-6"

FENCE

12"

6"

STEPS

Condominium & Mobile Home Space 5

A condominium is a multi-unit dwelling in which homeowners own their own units and the land directly underneath, and have joint ownership with other owners of all common property, such as walkways and parking areas. The landscaping around the complex is predetermined, but many condominium townhouses have a backyard or patio area or an atrium, and the apartment units usually have balconies for gardening. Generally, the patio or court is walled for privacy and is usually small. In any case, these areas afford the homeowner a place to garden at leisure.

The patio or allotted garden area is usually walled or fenced, and the homeowner must supply all soil and plant materials. A patio garden gives you greenery and offers low maintenance and care. It can be landscaped in several different ways, depending upon your personal taste and the dictates of time and money.

Balconies for gardening are usually small, but here is a perfect place to do container gardening. Growing plants in tubs and boxes is an easy way to let a few plants do a lot for you. Care is at a minimum and pleasure is at a maximum.

THE CONDO GARDEN

A patio or terrace needs careful planning because, even if it is used for only a few months in the year, it serves as another room. Before deciding what and where to plant, decide what kind of room you want it to be. The size and your personal needs will dictate what kind of outdoor living area you create. It can be a simple exposed patio, with plants adjacent to the home to make a handsome picture. If you enjoy outdoor cookery and dining, it can be a fully enclosed or partially roofed terrace convenient to the dining room or the kitchen. A terrace can also be an enclosed area off the bedroom, decorated with colorful flowering plants.

Pavings—The first consideration for the patio is the floor. Walls, if not already in place, ceilings, canopies, arbors and overhands can be built later. Look at all types of pavings at material supply yards and garden centers before making a decision. There is a wide selection of outdoor flooring materials. Choose carefully. Select a paving that is in character with your home. A patio floor may be concrete, but brick or flagstone is more dramatic, and tile gives long-lasting beauty.

Before making your final decision about the patio floor, ask yourself these questions:

- Will the paving withstand weather and wear?
- Will it be easy to maintain?
- Is the floor comfortable to walk on? Is it so rough that it might injure children's knees?
- Does water sink through the paving, or does it flow off in sheets, making it slippery?
- Should the paving be light colored or dark? Light paving creates a glare; dark paving stores up heat.
- Finally, think about the cost of materials and installation.

Concrete may not be as handsome as some other pavings, but it is durable, low-cost, and a very permanent surface. It is easy to clean, and if you object to its cold, gray look, mix it with color or cover it with paint or dye. Special paints are available which will seep deeply into the pores of the concrete. The concrete can also be rough or textured.

The slick, or hard finish is made by moving a steel trowel over the surface when it is partially hardened. Do the first troweling lightly, just enough to smooth the surface texture. Then trowel again with more pressure. This produces a floor that is slick, but somewhat uninteresting.

The wood-float method leaves a

Upper Right
Simple planters were made in the ground here by leaving bricks out of the paving pattern.

Center
Loose gravel and concrete smoothed with a wood float are brought together in this condominium garden. The olive tree and wooden planter benches make a handsome scene. Photo by Gary.

Lower Left
The white containers contrast nicely with the aggregate floor on these steps.

Lower Right
A wooden deck was laid over a concrete floor for this condominium garden. All the plants are in containers. Hanging pots add color and a sense of privacy.

floor smooth but not shiny. It is done with the mason's wood trowel, called a *float*.

The broom finish gives an interesting texture. It is made by brushing the slightly hardened concrete with a push broom.

Aggregate floor is made of concrete that has small stones on the surface. This creates a textured finish that is handsome and blends with plantings and lawns. The uneven texture breaks the monotony of a large area of paving, especially when it is framed with wood grids. The pebbly surface of aggregate concrete also eliminates glare and guarantees sure traction in wet weather. When this paving collects dirt, as it will, it is easy to clean with a strong hosing.

Brick is the most popular paving material, probably because it is difficult to commit a serious error when paving with it. By using the simple method of laying brick on sand, it is easy to take up the section and lay it again if the first attempt is not pleasing or accurate.

Brick comes in a variety of earthy colors that look good outdoors and give a pleasant contrast in texture. You can choose rough or smooth-surfaced brick, glazed or unglazed.

Besides blocks, other shapes are available too: hexagon, octagon, fleur-de-lis. Because the units are small, they never steal the show. They stay in scale with even the smallest foliage display.

There are many kinds of brick, but the best ones for patios are smooth-surfaced or rough-textured common brick. Face brick, including Roman and paving brick, is easier to work with and less expensive than slick brick. Common brick is usually available with pit marks on the surface. Sand-mold brick is smooth-textured and slightly larger on one face than on the other. Clinker brick has irregularities on the surface.

If you can, select hard-burned rather than green brick. It should be dark red in color rather than salmon, which indicates an under-burned process and less durability. Used or colored bricks are fine too. When you select the brick flooring be sure the dealer has a sufficient quantity to complete the area because there is usually some dimensional variation and color difference in later orders of brick. If you are in a climate where winters are severe, specify *SW* (severe weathering) brick.

Left
An outside fireplace surrounded by handsome planting creates an elegant setting for dining. Except for the small area on the right, all the planting in this garden is in containers. Photo by Max Eckert.

Right
Condominiums usually have limited space outdoors, but you can still create a lovely garden. Photo by Gary.

CONDOMINIUM GARDEN

1. PINUS THUNBERGII
2. PAXISTIMA CANBYI
3. PACHYSANDRA TERMINALIS

4. VINCA MINOR (BOWLES VARIETY)
5. ARCTOSTAPHYLOS UVA-URSI
6. AZALEA 'ELIZABETH'

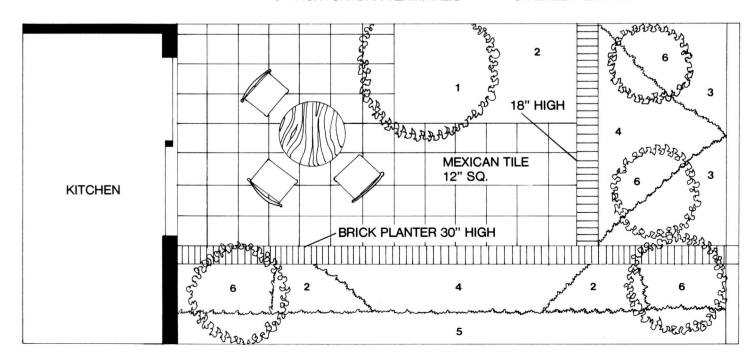

Bricks can be laid in a great variety of patterns—herringbone, basket weave, running bond, and so on—or combined with squares of grass or cinders in endless design. For large areas, the herringbone pattern looks best. Smaller patios look best with running bond or basket weave designs. Or break the large area by fitting bricks into redwood or cedar grid patterns. Bricks can also be set in mortar, but this is usually a job for the professional bricklayer.

Planning and Planting—You will find that a small condominium patio garden not only delights the eye but also means minimal gardening to keep you active and to create your own private Eden. And walled patio gardening is a delight to do. As your own special place, it is worth its space in gold.

As mentioned, a hard surface floor most likely will already have been installed by the contractor. If possible, have him leave planting pockets for plants. This breaks the monotony of a solid paved area and plants look good because they seem to belong rather than just being placed. Use one or two large planting pockets as accents for trees, perhaps. Place smaller planter beds along one wall for perennials and annuals. You do want plants in the patio, but you do not want a jungle if you plan to use the patio as an extra room for entertaining. A few specimen plants, a minimum of shrubbery, and a flower bed is really all that is required.

Plan your private garden with consideration of line and detail. In the outdoors, where there is a natural background, you can get away with a few mistakes, but not here. You will be working in a confined area, so look for plants with a little extra character. Take the time to search for that perfect olive tree with gnarled branches and sweeping graceful lines as an accent, or to select full bushy shrubs that will

add low horizontal thrust to the scene. A place to sit, some benches, and perhaps some statuary can transform a condominium garden into a visual treat you can be proud of. Provide seasonal color with perennials and annuals in suitable planters or in the spaces that have been left open in the paved area. Later you can add some stunning potted specimens for decoration outdoors in good weather and indoors in cold weather.

If the patio floor of your condominimum is already paved, you will be forced to use container plants, unless you want to dig up some paving. Plants in containers will allow you to decorate the area in little time. Select ornamental tubs and containers from the dozens now at suppliers. Choose small, graceful trees for shade and as accents. Grow bulbs, perennials and some annuals in planter boxes, which can be made from redwood as described in Chapter 6. This will add important seasonal color. Shrubs in containers look best when they are trimmed and pruned frequently, so be aware of this when planning the container garden. Once again, houseplants and trees of all kinds can be used in the patio in handsome tubs when weather permits and returned indoors for winter decoration.

Use line and balance within your patio, selecting vertical plants as well as low massing horizontal ones to balance the scene. For the best results, group planters and tubs together—say three tubs to an area—so

The use of boulders and a tree as a tall accent makes this mobile home entrance dramatic.

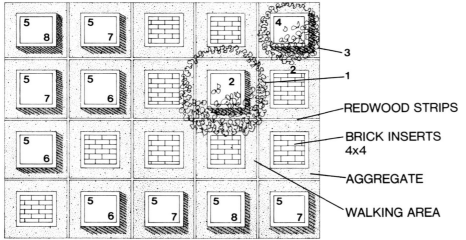

MODULAR GARDEN

1. WISTERIA FLORIBUNDA

2. HEDERA HELIX 'MANDA'S CRESTED CRINKLED IVY'

3. PAEONIA 'YACHIYOT SUBAKI'

4. DIANTHUS 'SNOWFLAKE'

5. ECHINACEA 'THE KING'

6. AGERATUM 'SUMMER SNOW'

7. BEGONIA 'WHITE CHRISTMAS'

8. VINCA 'LITTLE BLANCHE'

REDWOOD STRIPS

BRICK INSERTS 4x4

AGGREGATE

WALKING AREA

you can provide a good display. A lone tub can give a spotty effect. Groups of six to ten small pots with the same kind of plant are more effective than ten plants in one large tub. Search for really ornamental urns and jardinieres rather than the usual wooden ones. A certain amount of decorative flair is needed to make the patio garden a stellar one.

Caring for your plants in the patio garden is merely a question of sufficient watering and moderate feeding. Plants in tubs and boxes will need more water than those directly in the ground, and, in all cases, a sensible feeding and grooming program will keep everything in top shape. More details can be found in Chapter 12.

NARROW BALCONY GARDENS

Narrow balconies give the gardener little space for raising plants. Yet these long areas can be cleverly transformed into lush, green havens. It is not easy, but it can be done. Vines and trailers are essential to cover bare walls, to decorate railings, and, in some cases, to provide privacy from nearby neighbors. A small canvas or fiberglass awning is sometimes desirable, but you should first check with the building superintendent to see if this structure is allowed.

Pots of seasonal flowering plants are indispensable for balcony gardens. Rather than using one large pot, group several small ones together for a colorful display. If there is space, you might want window boxes on the sides of the balcony. A hanging basket on the wall, or perhaps two, adds another note of decoration. Often there is not enough space for much more on a narrow balcony. Yet even this small greenery is a welcome sight on a crowded street of brick buildings.

MOBILE HOMES

Mobile homes are apt to be confused with a trailer or camper. Actually, they are small factory-built houses delivered to a site. That they do have wheels to get them to the site has confused the issue somewhat. Once on the property, the mobile home is placed on a pier foundation and connected to water and electrical systems. There the home stays until the owner decides to move, in which case the wheels are attached and the home is moved somewhere else. More often, though, mobile homes are treated like permanent dwellings. They can be as large as 1,500 square feet, the size of an average house.

The major problem with mobile homes is that, once set on a piece of land, they appear out of place. Some kind of temporary or permanent landscaping is necessary to make them visually acceptable. At

first this may seem a chore, but one of my assistants who has a mobile home proved to me it is possible to transform these homes on wheels into a lovely picture. In a few months time she added a small grass area, pebbled paths, and some container plants.

Some mobile home parks have restrictions on planting, especially on permanant shrubs or trees. Also, utility lines are often laid underground and might be damaged by digging. Check with your park manager before planting.

A small lawn area around the sides and front of a mobile home will soften the severe looks. Lawns from seed do not cost much and will grow in a relatively short time.

Rather than put plants into the ground, put them in containers so they can be moved at will. Such a landscaping will offer enough greenery to make the total scene attractive. For privacy, hedges on each side of the mobile home may be a sound idea even though these must be in the ground. The cost will be well worth the expenditure. Small window boxes and planters are other added touches that can bring greenery to the mobile home. **Planning and Planting**—The best approach to planning a mobile home garden is to frame the house on three sides. This will make it an entity in itself. Plants can do the job for you better than anything else. Plants also provide privacy. Do not be afraid to use some tall hedge shrubs and an occasional small tree to give dimension to the site.

You can plant in the ground or use planter boxes, and you can grow almost any plant you want depending, of course, on climate. Keep the plan simple. Too many plants will require too much care and make the site seemed forced rather than attractive. A few well chosen plants, especially in specific areas, such as corners near the mobile house, can add great beauty.

Upper
Pots of azaleas and camellias accent this sideyard garden for a mobile home, and also act as a division between the homes.

Lower
The space around a mobile home is usually small, but a great deal can be accomplished with a few plants. Here the bark mulch contrasts nicely with the white gravel walkway.

Containers & Planters
6

Opposite
Wooden planters designed to fit these steps provide usable planting space and handsome decoration.

Below
Even a single container can be a striking addition to any garden.

Any garden, large or small, can use plants in containers. But, in a small space, containers can give you more growing area, help you control your fertilizer and water requirements, and let you simplify your gardening. And they let you put your plant exactly where you want it.

There are many types of containers on the market. Pots, planters and boxes are available at most nurseries. But the least expensive way to obtain containers is to design and build them yourself.

MAKING YOUR OWN

Any custom-made container should be constructed of redwood or cedar because these woods resist weathering. Construction-grade redwood which has some defects is fine. You can also use pine or Douglas fir if you protect the wood with a preservative or paint.

If you do not want to cut the wood for your containers yourself, tell the lumber dealer the size of boards or pieces you need and he will cut the wood for you. Order the wood by thickness, width and length, in that order. For example, you can order a 2x6x8-foot board. It should be 2 inches thick by 6 inches wide by 8 feet long, but lumber sizes are not true. A standard 2x4, for instance, is actually 1-1/2 by 3-1/2 inches. The chart on page 89 gives nominal and actual dimensions. Pieces smaller than 2 by 4 inches are usually called *strips* or 2x3s or 1x2s.

Next, specify the type and grade of wood you want. Construction-grade is fine for most containers.

If you can put a nail into wood, you can build your own boxes and planters. The design of the box will depend on its size—small boxes, large boxes and long planters are easily made. They are nothing more than four sides and a bottom nailed at the corners.

Drainage holes are essential in all boxes so excess water can run off. Drill directly into the box or use plastic liners with holes punched in the bottom of the plastic. How you stack the boxes depends on how much space is available. They can be put in levels or used on the ground. Stacked boxes, of course, are at a higher level and easier to tend. Put the boxes anywhere on the porch, patio or balcony. The illustrations in this book suggest some of the numerous arrangements possible for containers.

DETAILING CONTAINERS

If you do not like the look of bare wood, add detailing to the containers. Use wood strips latticework or diamond patterns on the outsides of containers. This detailing puts the finishing touches on the containers and adds a note of elegance. The detailing of the outside of a container depends mainly on the container's size, so proportion and symmetry should be considered. For example, detail large containers with big strips of wood; detail smaller containers with smaller pieces or strips of woods.

One effective outside-the-container motif is a raised rectangle outlining the container, which creates a shadowbox effect. For the average container this design requires 16 pieces of 1 by 2-inch strips of wood, four pieces for each side. Nail or glue the strips about 1/2 inch in from edges of the box. Another method is to place strips of wood vertically or horizontally 1/2 inch apart. This will add flair to the basic box and cover construction mistakes.

When you detail a wood container, you should always add a molding or *cap* at the top edge a finished look. Caps usually are 1 by 3 inches. Nail them in place, letting the outer edge overhand the container by 1/2 to 1 inch.

You can also score a container with a wood chisel. A basic pattern consists of 1/2-inch deep knife cuts spaced 1/2 to 1 inch apart, vertically or horizontally, on the container. This design creates a bas-relief look. Rent a sanding machine or sand the wood by hand to a lustrous smooth finish.

Upper
Containers don't have to be exactly alike to work together. It is more pleasing if they are made of the same material, though.

Lower
Of course, containers don't have to stay outdoors. For less hardy plants that need to be indoors during winter, containers are ideal. Further details are in Chapter 9.

Opposite Page
Containers and terracing are combined in this stunning garden. The area is only about 15 by 15 feet.

PLANTERS

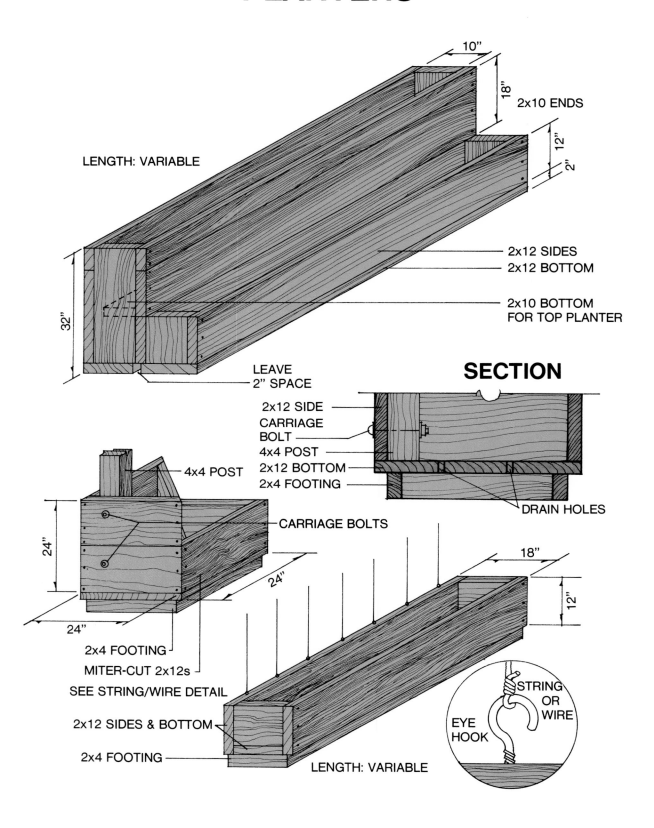

10"

18"

2x10 ENDS

12"

2"

LENGTH: VARIABLE

2x12 SIDES

2x12 BOTTOM

2x10 BOTTOM
FOR TOP PLANTER

32"

LEAVE
2" SPACE

SECTION

2x12 SIDE

CARRIAGE
BOLT

4x4 POST

2x12 BOTTOM

2x4 FOOTING

DRAIN HOLES

4x4 POST

CARRIAGE BOLTS

24"

24"

24"

18"

12"

2x4 FOOTING

MITER-CUT 2x12s

SEE STRING/WIRE DETAIL

2x12 SIDES & BOTTOM

2x4 FOOTING

LENGTH: VARIABLE

STRING
OR
WIRE

EYE
HOOK

TRIANGLE PLANTER

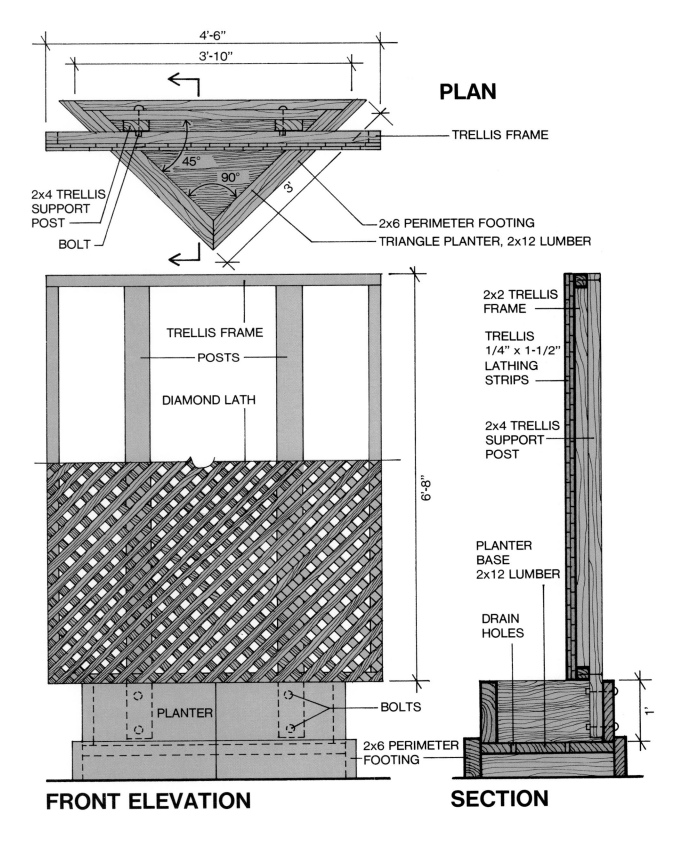

PLAN

4'-6"

3'-10"

TRELLIS FRAME

45°

90°

3'

2x4 TRELLIS SUPPORT POST

BOLT

2x6 PERIMETER FOOTING

TRIANGLE PLANTER, 2x12 LUMBER

TRELLIS FRAME

POSTS

DIAMOND LATH

6'-8"

2x2 TRELLIS FRAME

TRELLIS 1/4" x 1-1/2" LATHING STRIPS

2x4 TRELLIS SUPPORT POST

PLANTER BASE 2x12 LUMBER

DRAIN HOLES

PLANTER

BOLTS

1'

2x6 PERIMETER FOOTING

FRONT ELEVATION

SECTION

PLANTERS

Planters usually are long and narrow or shaped like a window-box. Give the design of the planter some thought; small planters coordinate with small plants, large ones with big plants. You should elevate planters with 2-inch blocks under each corner so air can enter the box from underneath.

Build planters from construction-grade redwood, as noted earlier. The redwood will eventually turn a lovely silver color. Make planters from 2x4s, 1x12s or 2x12s. A good size container is 12 inches wide, 10 inches deep and 36 inches long.

MODULAR GARDENS

Similar to container gardening, and perhaps it can be included in that term, modular gardening is growing plants in boxes and arranging the boxes in appealing groups. The boxes—squares, rectangles, parallelograms—are placed side by side to carry out endless patterns. For small areas, this is a highly effective way to use plants. Plants in handsome boxes are more dramatic, and the size of the garden is forgotten in the beauty of the patterns created with the boxes. Further, this portable garden provides color and accent where and when you want it in the landscape. It is an easy form of gardening; no weeding, mulching or exacting care is needed.

A modular garden can be set up on a deck, patio or any place within the property. Besides its visual appeal, a modular approach gives the homeowner a chance to enjoy a garden even if the soil on his property will not support plants.

The somewhat formal geometric patterns created by the planter boxes are best suited to a contemporary house or formal architecture. For a rustic or cottage home, a garden in standard pots and tubs is more suitable.

Successful modular gardens de-pend on the right combination of different-sized boxes. Vary both the heights and the widths of the boxes. Butt them together or line them against a fence; use them in an L-shaped pattern or in a herringbone design. Remember, it is the combination of boxes that makes the modular concept work. If one arrangement is not pleasing, move the boxes around until you find the right treatment for the area. The pattern created by the boxes is the basic design of your garden.

BOXES

Flats are wooden boxes that nurseries use to grow seedlings. They consist of four sides and a bottom. Modular boxes are similarly designed. You will have to build boxes at home because commercial planters probably will not work, but boxes are easy projects. The dimensions will vary for each box, so draw your entire plan on paper before you start construction.

Redwood is the best material. As I mentioned in the previous chapter, it needs no preservatives and will last for years. Douglas fir is stronger than redwood, but more costly. It is best for boxes over 16 inches square, and it needs a protective coating to prevent rotting. Glue and screw all corners of wood containers, or nail them together securely. Use 1-inch stock for most boxes, 2-inch boards for larger ones.

Containers clustered together can give the feel of a large garden.

Opposite Page
Although there are several different kinds of containers in this small space, they were all chosen to match the character of this Arizona garden.

You can build all kinds of boxes. Small boxes, 3 inches deep, are perfect for small bulbs and annuals. Medium sizes are best for shrubs and specimen plants. Use boxes 24 inches square for trees. What goes into the box determines how deep it should be. Be sure that the bottom boards are placed 1/4 inch apart so excess water can drain freely.

PLANTING IN CONTAINERS OR BOXES

Almost any plant can be grown in a box temporarily. Some plants, such as camellias and azaleas, do better in a container where roots are confined and the size of the plant does not become cumbersome. With a box it is possible to cater to the plants exact needs for the right soil and light. Prepare the soil for the boxes carefully. This is about all you have to do to start the garden.

Put a 2-inch bed of small stones

or chipped gravel in a 12x16-inch box and scatter a few lumps of charcoal over the bed. The charcoal will help keep the soil sweet.

For most plants, fill the box to about 1/2 inch from the top with a mix of equal parts of top soil from your garden and humus, or use one of the many commercial soil mixes available.

Plant your plants as you usually would. Water the plants thoroughly after planting and attend to them the first few weeks until they be-come established. Then they can grow on their own, as long as they receive adequate moisture.

Place the box according to your landscape plan. Large containers and tubs can be moved on dollies.

ANNUALS

Most annuals, commonly available at nurseries, are ideal for modular gardens because their roots are shallow. Boxes of annuals add immediate color to a terrace or garden, and, with proper care, they will bloom for a long time. Low-growing annuals like petunias give stellar splashes of concentrated color. Tall ones like *Celosia plumosa* are excellent for vertical accent against a terrace wall or a fence. Several boxes of rail lillies, *Schizanthus,* are charming on the patio or terrace.

You can mix annuals, too. Several different annuals in a redwood box,

green leaves and erect spikes of white and lilac flowers in green bracts. It blooms easily with little care, but needs a large tub.

Campanula isophylla, the bell-flower, has blue star-shaped flowers. It is a small plant that looks well in an ornate container. It needs plenty of water and partial shade.

Chrysanthemums are excellent for autumn because of the many sizes and colors available. Many varieties flower as late as November. Pinch back plants in early part of season and be sure that soil is always moderately wet. Sunshine is best, although some varieties bloom in partial shade. Chrysanthemums are well suited to low, standard clay pots or white shallow bowls.

There are many varieties of geranium. The 'Lady Washington' varieties have dark green, heart-shaped leaves and pink, red, lavender, or white flowers with and without markings. The garden geranium is *Pelargonium hortorum*. It has round leaves with scalloped margins, often with a colored zone in center. Single or double flowers are available in shades of white, pink, red or salmon. Groups of potted geraniums around posts, at entrances, or at terrace corners are handsome. A very large, low tub filled with many geraniums is equally attractive.

Several species of *Helleborus,* such as the Christmas-rose, *Helleborus niger,* or the Lenten rose, *Helleborus orientalis*, are good for boxes and tubs.

Hosta, the plantain lily, is big, and has lush green leaves. It is a very decorative plant for difficult areas because it often blooms in dense shade. Easy to grow; best in squatty tubs.

Lantana is a robust, hard-to-kill plant that bears many orange and red flowers month after month. Give it full sunlight and rather dry soil. Trailing lantana, *Lantana montevidensis,* has purple flowers and is especially nice for hanging baskets.

for example, a bouquet of balsam in the center surrounded by vivid blue lobelia, can be stunning. Annuals can provide a constant flow of color all summer. If you want a delicious fragrance, try nicotiana placed in tapered bowls.

Most annuals should be planted in a good general potting mix. Feed plants biweekly. Water them heavily on warm days and be sure that they get some sunshine. There are many varieties available, but some of my favorites are listed here. Additional annuals are listed on page 131.

Browallia speciosa has an amethyst flower with small, violet white-throated flowers. It needs bright light and copious water. Blooms through spring and summer.

Cineraria has lovely blue, purple, red, crimson, and white flowers. It blooms freely in partial shade and coolness and looks best in low, standard clay pots.

Impatiens includes many varieties with double flowers in pink, white or lavender. Give plants sunlight and feeding. They are handsome in tubs or boxes.

Lobelia has vivid blue flowers, although there is also a pale blue variety. Color lasts through summer

and fall. These are excellent small plants.

All kinds of petunias are easy to grow. They bloom for months in a wide range of colors: white, purple, pink, lavender, red and yellow. Dwarf, trailing and large ruffled varieties are available. Give sunlight and water. For a really stunning effect, grow a mass of one variety in a large cube-shaped redwood container.

Many species and varieties of primrose are available in pink, lavender or white. They are nice for window boxes and border decoration. They like some shade.

PERENNIALS
Perennials provide continuous summer color. Geraniums, tuberous begonias, and chrysanthemums are only a few of the many available.

All perennials must have a rest period sometime during the year. Those that bloom in summer rest over the winter. Winter blooming plants rest in summer. The season of bloom depends on your individual climate. Here are some varieties you may want to consider.

Acanthus mollis, the Grecian urn plant, is large, with rosettes of dark

Tuberous *begonias* have spectacular flowers in a wide range of colors with single, double, ruffled, camellia and rose forms. These plants need coolness and are difficult to grow in heat. Excellent for hanging redwood containers.

BULBS

Potted bulbs offer early spring color, a succession of bloom through many months, and are lovely in a modular garden.

Many spring bulbs can be planted in the late fall. The containers should be stored over winter in a cool dark shaded spot such as a basement or pantry. They can be brought into the house in early winter. The leaves will be pale yellow and white from a lack of light, but foliage turns green and growth starts in a matter of days with bright sunlight. When it is warm enough outside, move the bulbs to the terrace or patio.

After they flower take the bulbs back inside, but don't cut off the foliage. Keep it growing until the leaves begin to yellow, and then gradually let the soil dry. When the foliage and soil are dry, lift the bulbs from the container and store them in brown paper sacks in a cool place for fall planting.

A good soil mix for bulbs is three parts garden loam, one part sand, and one part leaf mold. To start bulbs, cover the bottom of the container with pebbles. Fill the pot about one-third full of soil, and set the bulbs on top. Fill soil in and around until tips are barely covered. For a concentration of color, plant bulbs close together.

Achimenes gives pretty color from charming small plants. Plants come in a variety of colors. All need sunlight and plenty of water.

Autumn crocus have dramatic tulip-shaped flowers in brilliant yellow, lavender or rose color. Several planted in a redwood box or shallow clay pot make a showy display in August and September. Keep them quite wet in partial shade. For contrast, set crocuses in pots on brick floors or against paved walls.

Many varieties of daffodil bloom from January to May. Most of the easy-to-grow varieties sparkle with color in planters and window boxes. Plant bulbs in late fall. When growth starts, move them to sunshine and keep them liberally watered.

Hyacinths give much color for little effort. They are hardy bulbs with bright green leaves and fragrant flowers in white, pink or blue. They need lots of sunlight and water, and bloom in March and April.

Nurseries stock mature Kaffir lilies in pots for spring bloom. They are very dramatic with clusters of vivid orange or red flowers. The Kaffir lily deserves a pot on the terrace. It looks grand in large round tubs and can be grown in the same container for several years.

CORNER GARDENS

A corner can be a special place for a diminutive garden. I have created many tiny greeneries in barren corners on my property and these little spaces deserve mention. It is easy to install a corner garden in a weekend and if you have very little space, this can become a sylvan spot, tiny though it may be.

Use stacked boxes or terracing as shown in our drawings to create this unique garden. You can grow annuals, perennials and bulbs. You can even grow a few small shrubs. This little extra garden can be incorporated in the overall plan or it can be a separate entity.

You can grow almost any kind of plant in a planter, pot or box. There are few limitations. In Chapter 11 you will find a list of annuals, perennials, bulbs, shrubs, trees, and some fine vines for your rooftop, patio, balcony or porch garden. The list is only partial; there are hundreds of plants you can grow, but these are some of the ones most likely to succeed.

Opposite Page
This large wooden box gives both greenery and color.

CORNER GARDEN

POST PLANTER BOTTOM, DRILL DRAIN HOLES

PLANTER POST, 8' LONG, CONCRETE COLLAR

PLANTER SIDES, 2x12s

POSTS, TOP END BEVELLED

PLANTER SUPPORT, 2x6s, BOLTED TO POST

BOLTS

TOP TERRACE POST, SET IN GROUND 18"

TERRACE ENDS, 2x12s

TERRACE POSTS, BOLTED TO TERRACE

TERRACE BOTTOM LINES, UNDERGROUND

TREAT ALL SUNKEN POSTS WITH SUITABLE WOOD PRESERVATIVE. LUMBER SPECIES: REDWOOD ROUGH, OR SIMILAR DECAY-RESISTANT SPECIES.

CONSTRUCTION DETAILS

CORNER GARDEN

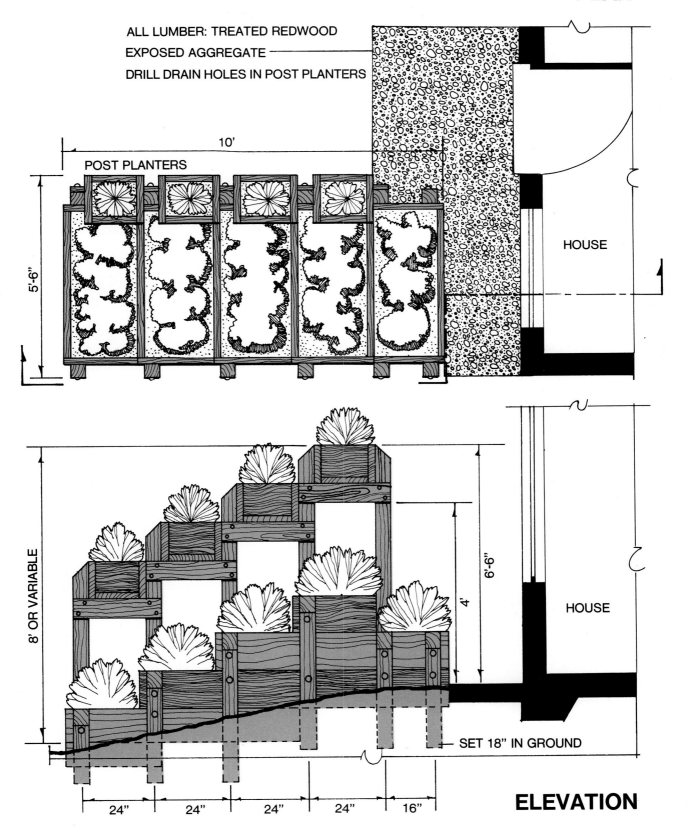

PLAN

ALL LUMBER: TREATED REDWOOD

EXPOSED AGGREGATE

DRILL DRAIN HOLES IN POST PLANTERS

10'

POST PLANTERS

5'-6"

HOUSE

8' OR VARIABLE

6'-6"

4'

HOUSE

SET 18" IN GROUND

24"   24"   24"   24"   16"

ELEVATION

Vertical Gardens: Growing Food

7

Vegetables, fruits and berries can be grown horizontally only on acres of land, but in a small garden, you can grow these gems vertically on fences, trellises, posts, walls or in containers. In fact, squash, cucumbers, berries and peas grow *better* vertically. The trellises, posts and containers can be placed anywhere: on the patio, on a side fence, or on your balcony. If your present space is, say 5 by 5 feet, you can, with perhaps only two trellises and a fence, increase the growing space to 100 square feet. The only thing to remember when gardening vertically is that your soil must be specially prepared—it has to have plenty of nutrients so the plants will thrive as discussed in Chapter 8.

CONSTRUCTION KNOW-HOW

Besides the vine clamps, eyebolts, hangers and wire mesh, which you can buy, you will need posts, trellises and other supports so plants have something to grasp or cling to. The construction of these items is not at all difficult, if you follow our plans.

POSTS

Use redwood, cedar or treated pine 2x4s to make your posts. Nail chicken wire or laths onto the posts lengthwise, ladder-style, every 8 to 12 inches. As I mentioned in the preceding chapter, lathing is redwood or cedar strips 3/8 by 1-5/8 inches. Use *surface lath,* which is relatively free of knotholes and blemishes. In a sideyard, sink posts 18 inches into the soil; if the posts are on a patio, balcony or other area without natural soil, bolt the posts to railing or walls with L clamps.

Start plants in planters or containers placed at the bottom of the posts using the methods described in Chapter 8. Soon you can start training the plants to the lathing or wire. Ideal choices are tomatoes, eggplant, squash and peas. Four posts will enable you to grow enough

of these vegetables to feed your entire family.

FENCES

If you have an existing fence in your yard, half your work is done. You can make a box garden on the fence by hanging planter boxes on brackets at varying levels. The average small fence will hold three 36-inch planters spaced 20 inches apart horizontally. This box garden is perfect for beets, carrots and lettuce.

You can also run wire in a grid pattern directly on the fence, but be sure to leave 12 to 16 inches between wires. Start vining vegetables like squash and peas at the bottom of the fence in planter boxes or in the ground. Another excellent planting plan, if you have room, involves runing a partition at right angles to the fence. This gives you more surfaces on which to grow plants. Cover some surfaces with construction or baling wire or trellises; use planter boxes for root crops on other surfaces.

BUILDING A TRELLIS

Trellises are generally made of standard 1-5/8-inch-wide lathing available in bundles ot 50 pieces. The most satisfactory lathing is made of redwood or red cedar heartwood. These woods are decay-resistant and therefore resist rotting due to rain and contact with the soil. Their straight grain makes them less likely to warp. You also can use pine or fir lathing, but if you do, apply some protective coating to the wood to protect it. Finally, you can also make trellises from tree branches. Use any durable, somewhat flexible wood; just remember to remove any stems and twigs. Fasten together large poles or other woods with strong wire at the junctions.

One method of making a trellis consists of nailing and epoxying one lath on another in a cross pattern. If you need much strength use the *interlocking method.*

FENCE GARDEN

PLAN

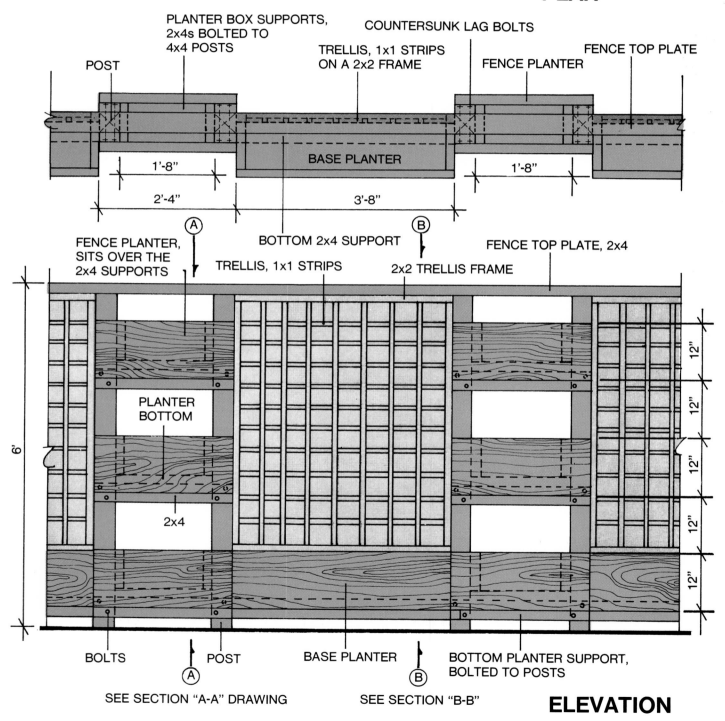

PLANTER BOX SUPPORTS,
2x4s BOLTED TO
4x4 POSTS

COUNTERSUNK LAG BOLTS

TRELLIS, 1x1 STRIPS
ON A 2x2 FRAME

FENCE PLANTER

FENCE TOP PLATE

POST

BASE PLANTER

1'-8"

2'-4"

3'-8"

1'-8"

Ⓐ

Ⓑ

FENCE PLANTER,
SITS OVER THE
2x4 SUPPORTS

BOTTOM 2x4 SUPPORT

FENCE TOP PLATE, 2x4

TRELLIS, 1x1 STRIPS

2x2 TRELLIS FRAME

PLANTER
BOTTOM

2x4

6'

12"

12"

12"

12"

12"

BOLTS

POST

BASE PLANTER

BOTTOM PLANTER SUPPORT,
BOLTED TO POSTS

Ⓐ

Ⓑ

SEE SECTION "A-A" DRAWING

SEE SECTION "B-B"

ELEVATION

FENCE GARDEN

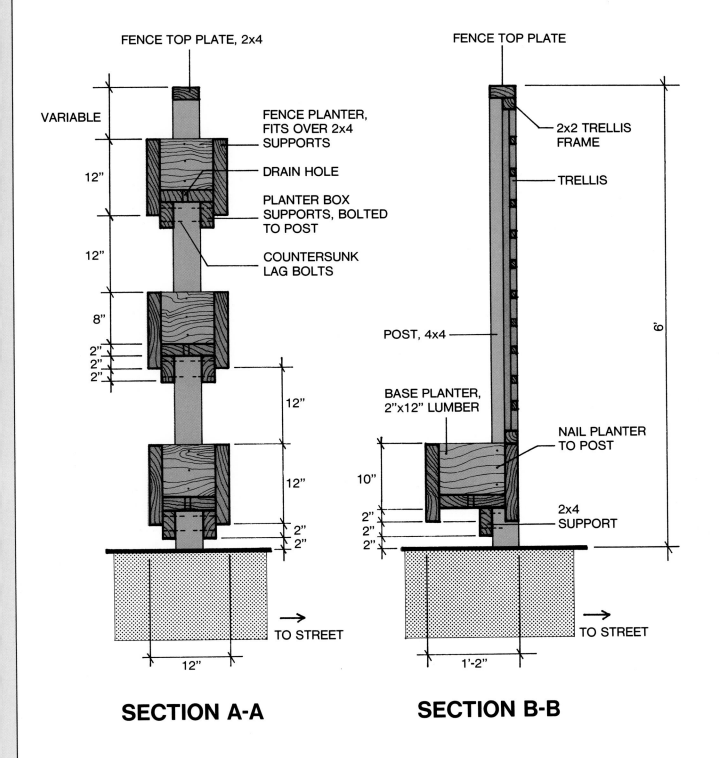

SECTION A-A

FENCE TOP PLATE, 2x4

VARIABLE

12"

12"

8"

2"
2"
2"

FENCE PLANTER,
FITS OVER 2x4
SUPPORTS

DRAIN HOLE

PLANTER BOX
SUPPORTS, BOLTED
TO POST

COUNTERSUNK
LAG BOLTS

12"

12"

2"
2"

12"

→ TO STREET

SECTION B-B

FENCE TOP PLATE

2x2 TRELLIS
FRAME

TRELLIS

POST, 4x4

6'

BASE PLANTER,
2"x12" LUMBER

NAIL PLANTER
TO POST

10"

2"
2"
2"

2x4
SUPPORT

→ TO STREET

1'-2"

3'x3' TRELLIS GARDEN

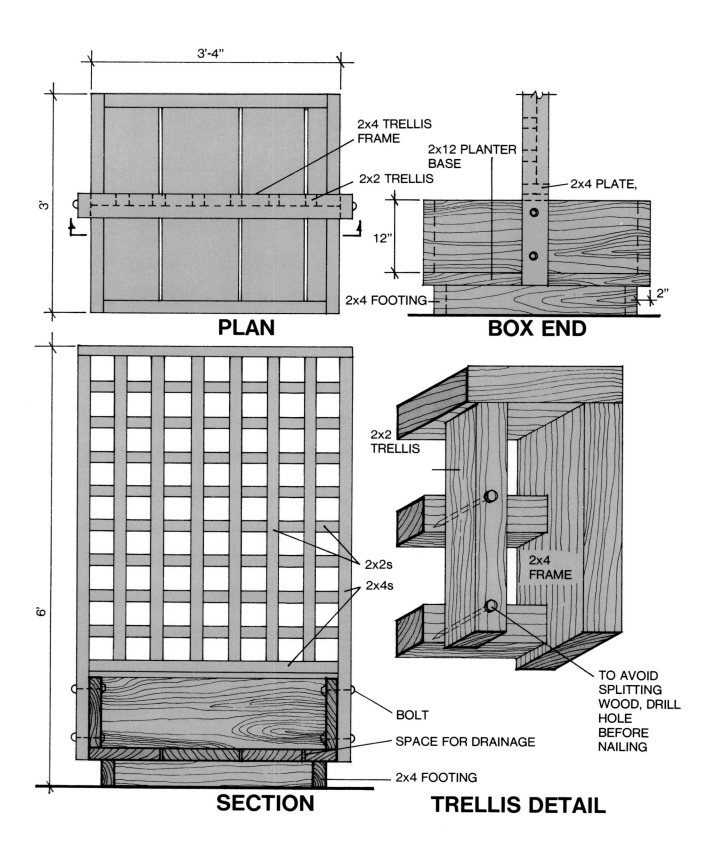

3'-4"

2x4 TRELLIS FRAME

2x2 TRELLIS

3'

PLAN

2x12 PLANTER BASE

2x4 PLATE,

12"

2x4 FOOTING

2"

BOX END

6'

2x2s

2x4s

BOLT

SPACE FOR DRAINAGE

2x4 FOOTING

SECTION

2x2 TRELLIS

2x4 FRAME

TO AVOID SPLITTING WOOD, DRILL HOLE BEFORE NAILING

TRELLIS DETAIL

TRELLIS DESIGNS

GRID DESIGN

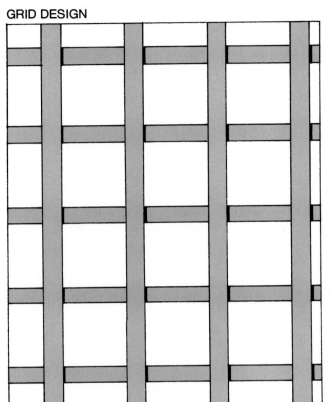

DIAMOND DESIGN

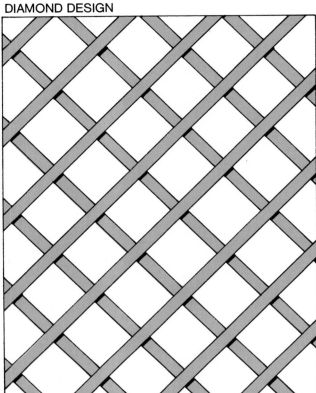

HERRINGBONE DESIGN

LUMBER SIZES

When you plan any wood project, be sure you allow for the difference between the size you order and the actual size you will get.

Kiln-Dried Lumber

Size to Order	Actual Size in Inches
1x4	3/4 by 3-1/2
1x6	3/4 by 5-1/2
1x8	3/4 by 7-1/4
2x4	1-1/2 by 3-1/3
2x6	1-1/2 by 5-1/2
2x8	1-1/2 by 7-1/4

Unseasoned Boards

Size to Order	Actual Size in Inches
1x3	25/32 by 2-9/16
1x4	25/32 by 3-9/16
1x6	25/32 by 5-5/8
1x8	25/32 by 7-1/4
2x3	1-9/16 by 2-9/16
2x4	1-9/16 by 3-9/16
2x6	1-9/16 by 5-5/8
2x8	1-9/16 by 7-1/2
2x10	1-9/16 by 9-1/2

INTERLOCKING

The interlocking method of construction uses 1x1s, 2x2s and 2x4s. First tape together bundles of 2 by 2-inch strips, ten pieces to a bundle, with the ends flush. Next, mark across all these pieces with parallel, 1-inch wide lines. Space the lines evenly. Now place masking tape lengthwise on your saw at a 1-inch depth for sawing the 2-inch strips. Saw down as far as the tape, just inside your markings. Take a small hammer and strike between the saw cuts to knock out the chunk of wood, leaving a socket or groove. Insert 1 by 1-inch wood strips crossways into the grooves. They should fit flush. Now make a frame from 2x4s. Nail strips into grooved pieces and, to finish, paint the trellis. Or leave it natural. Either way, it will be both functional and attractive.

Spacing Laths—In any method of constructing a trellis the spacing of laths is important for three reasons; (1) to create a definite pattern, (2) to allow plants sufficient room to grasp wood, and (3) for shadow and light patterns. For lath 1/2 inch or less thick, space laths 3/4 inch apart. For lath 1/2 inch to 1 inch thick, use a 3/4-inch space. For lath 2 by 2 inches thick, 1- to 2-inch spacing works well. Spacing must be consistent because any variation will be noticeable.

Using a Spacer—Use a spacer—a wooden block—between the laths as you nail them in place. Lay the spacer flat on top as you nail the

lath in place; lay it flat near the bottom when you nail the bottom of the lath in place. Use *lathing nails,* sold at hardware stores, to nail one piece of lath over another piece. Use regular galvanized-metal nails for the framing. For extra strength, use a wood epoxy in addition to the nails. The drawings on page 89 show detailed plans of several trellis patterns.

BUYING A TRELLIS

Commercially made trellises come in large, open or boxed, rectangular, square, fan or canopy-shaped designs. Commercial trellises are usually made of 1/8-inch stock in several heights, sizes and qualities. These trellises usually do not last more than a few years. Also, they are not very attractive and you are limited to using the sizes available.

PLANTING

The vertical garden is the place to have your vegetable garden. These gardens-in-the-air work perfectly for many vegetables because so many of them are vining or climbing types—tomatoes, cucumbers, squash, peas and many others. You can certainly grow flower gardens vertically, too.

You also can grow fruit trees vertically with great success. Most berries are climbers and therefore very suitable to vertical gardening.

PLANNING YOUR VEGETABLE GARDEN

You will not need a large plot of ground for trellis vegetable gardening. Even if you have only a walkway and fence, you can grow some vegetables in planters, or wherever you can erect a trellis. If you have space, use the ground area for root crops like beets and carrots and, as I mentioned, grow vining crops on trellises or fences or walls.

Do not try to do too much the first year. Put in a few crops for trellis gardening and enjoy them rather than attempt to grow so many vegetables that gardening becomes a chore.

You can grow vegetables directly in the ground parallel to fences or walls—wherever you can erect a trellis—or you can use planters. Just what you do depends on the space and the character of the garden area. If you have only a patio, it is far better to garden in containers. If there is a small garden area where you are growing other plants, then growing in the ground with trellis support may harmonize better with the overall scheme.

In your space saving trellis gardens you can grow many vining crops. The ones discussed here will get you started.

BEANS

Pole beans are an ideal crop for trellis gardening. They love to climb and a good harvest depends on tall lush plants. Don't confuse pole beans with snap beans which grow into small bushes. Pole beans have more flavor and usually are more productive than the bush beans. Dig deep generous holes and use a rich soil with some compost added to it. Fertilize beans with a vegetable food and grow with plenty of water. This is a spring and summer crop, and seed should be planted about 1 inch deep.

Pole beans produce in 60 to 70 days and can be picked at various stages of growth. The pods usually are ready about three weeks after blooms. If plants are healthy, you can pick beans every three to five days.

PEPPERS

Peppers are not true vining plants, but rather are bushy plants with dark green foliage. However, they can be grown easily in containers with trellises or in the ground with trellises as supports, or on fences or walls. These plants need a warm growing period of about two months, when night temperatures never drop below 65°F (19°C). Start planting in April or May, depending upon your region.

You can also grow long and slender hot peppers or the succulent sweet bell peppers. Peppers make attractive, bushy, 2- to 3-feet tall plants for patio, terrace, or porch decoration. Harvest them eight to nine weeks after the first transplanting. Frequent harvesting will encourage production throughout the summer.

EGGPLANT

Eggplant does best at about 80°F (25°C) during the day and 68°F (20°C) at night. Start seeds in April or May, depending upon your location, or buy prestarted plants. Eggplant needs a long and warm growing season. Keep well watered and well lit.

Plants are easily trained to trellises and grow 3 to 4 feet tall,

Opposite Page, Left
Fruit trees in background are espaliered on trellises to increase growing space. Note space between trellises and wall. This allows air to flow on all sides of the plant.

Opposite Page, Right
Productive vegetable garden relies on vertical structures for growing space. Site is only a few feet wide.

1'x4' POST GARDEN

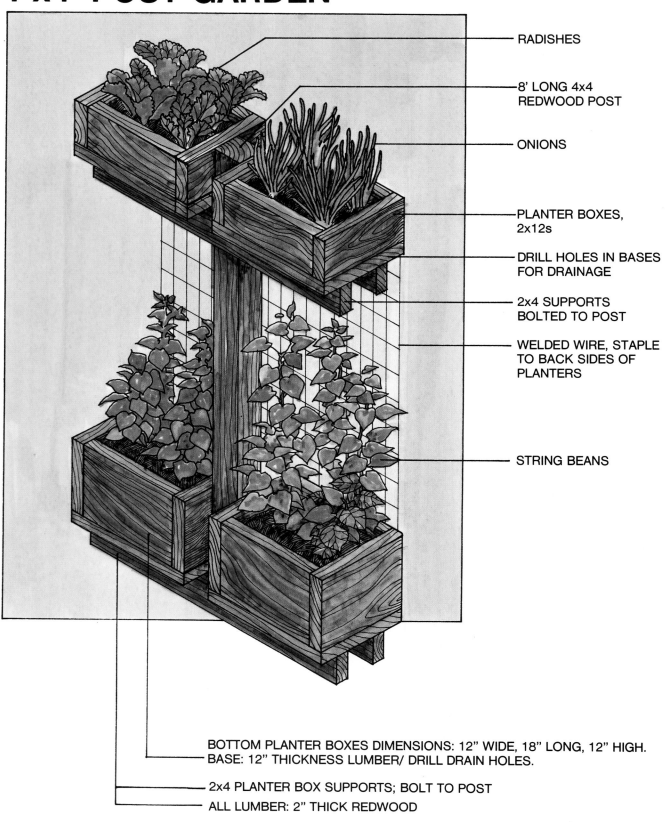

RADISHES

8' LONG 4x4 REDWOOD POST

ONIONS

PLANTER BOXES, 2x12s

DRILL HOLES IN BASES FOR DRAINAGE

2x4 SUPPORTS BOLTED TO POST

WELDED WIRE, STAPLE TO BACK SIDES OF PLANTERS

STRING BEANS

BOTTOM PLANTER BOXES DIMENSIONS: 12" WIDE, 18" LONG, 12" HIGH.
BASE: 12" THICKNESS LUMBER/ DRILL DRAIN HOLES.

2x4 PLANTER BOX SUPPORTS; BOLT TO POST

ALL LUMBER: 2" THICK REDWOOD

1'x4' POST GARDEN

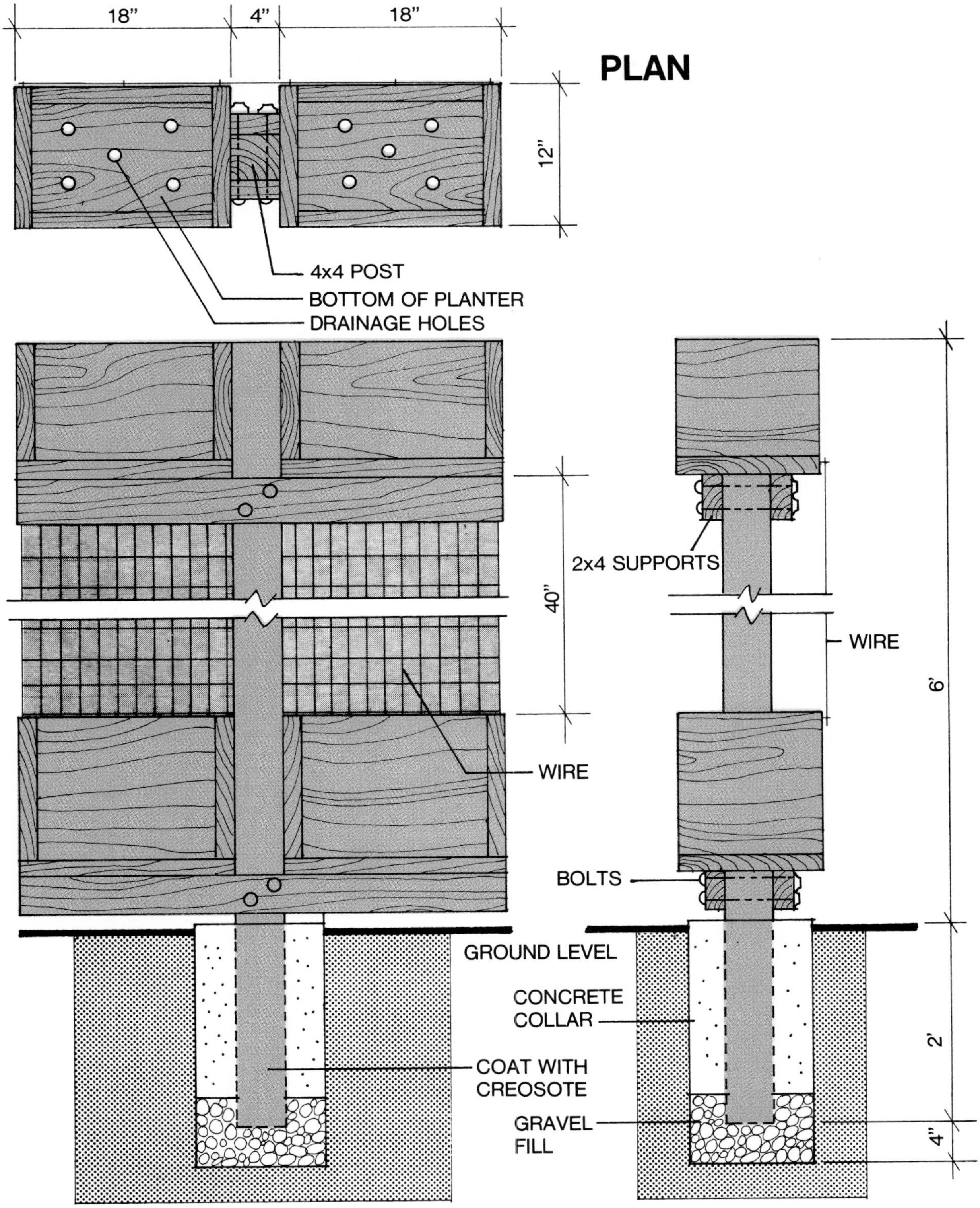

18"   **4"**   **18"**

12"

PLAN

4x4 POST
BOTTOM OF PLANTER
DRAINAGE HOLES

40"

2x4 SUPPORTS

WIRE

WIRE

6'

BOLTS

GROUND LEVEL

CONCRETE COLLAR

COAT WITH CREOSOTE

GRAVEL FILL

2'

4"

FRONT ELEVATION

SIDE ELEVATION

CONSTRUCTION DETAILS

depending upon the variety. Remove some blossoms as they appear so your eggplant does not set too many fruits. Pinch back terminal stem growth to keep the plant bushy. Eggplant should bear fruit in 75 to 90 days; harvest immediately, even when the fruits are half size. If picked late, they will have a bitter taste.

CUCUMBERS

Cucumbers are extremely robust and grow quickly. These vines are ideal for trellis gardening. You can sow seed directly in soil in a large 12-inch container or in the ground. Insert trellises so the plant can climb. Train the vine so the center becomes bushy and lateral stems develop sideways.

Give plants plenty of water and be sure to add some manure to the soil. Keep plants in a bright place, although direct sun is not necessary. Cucumbers start bearing in about 40 to 70 days and can be picked at any stage. The young ones will be tiny, but ideal for sweet pickles. Larger cucumbers, if you let them mature, are fine for salads.

TOMATOES

There are few foods that beat the sweet luscious taste of freshly picked tomatoes. There are midget varieties specifically for container growing which, nevertheless, will still need a trellis, and standard varieties for soil planting. You can start your own plants from seed, but many people buy prestarted seedlings because there is a good selection available.

Tomatoes need warm temperatures and as much sun as possible to produce a good crop. Tomatoes are climbers and trellises keep them from becoming a jungle. Tie plants to the wood members with plastic or paper covered wire ties. Do not tie them so tightly you cut the stems, however.

Give the plants plenty of water and good feeding with any of the several tomato-type foods sold at nurseries. Keep the plants growing continuously so you have a good harvest. Fertilize first about a week after you transplant the seedlings and again 2 weeks later. While plants are producing fruit, fertilize every week.

If there are no bees in the area, you can pollinate tomato blossoms by shaking the plant. To be effective, flower clusters must be near the top of the plant. Midday, when the temperature is warm, and the humidity low, is the best time to shake the plant. New blossoms open daily over a period of time. Keep tomatoes at temperatures above 60°F (15°C) at night or they may not set fruit. Very warm temperatures, over 95°F (35°C), also will affect plants adversely, so shelter plants from extreme sun on very hot days.

Thin tomato plants by removing the small *suckers* as they form. These are the tiny first two or three leaves that appear between the main stem and the foliage. Depending upon the variety, tomatoes should bear within 70 to 80 days after seed planting.

PEAS

Fresh garden peas are easy to grow. Plant in spring as soon as the soil is dry. You can sow peas again in mid-summer to have a second harvest in fall. Peas need a soil that has good porosity because they have long roots. They also need support—a trellis works beautifully for them. If temperatures get too hot you will have all vines and no pods. Pick pods regularly; left on the vine too long they become hard. Plant seeds a dozen to a square foot of space, 1-1/2 inches deep. Peas mature in 60 to 70 days and while they are germinating they need plenty of water; later they do not need as much but keep the soil moist.

Watch for aphids which cause stunted, curly leaves on plants.

PUMPKIN

I don't know how utilitarian pumpkins are in the scheme of things, but I do know they are fun to grow. Often, however, you get too many, all a family needs is one or two—for piemaking or seeds.

The pumpkin, a vining plant, does well on trellises, but be sure the wood supports are strong enough to hold the weight of the plant. Use a good soil enriched with compost and select a sunny site for the pumpkins; plant seeds 18 to 24 inches apart and when vines start, thin them out so two strong ones remain and train these to the trellis. Provide plenty of water; pumpkins need about 100 growing days for maturity.

I would hardly suggest pumpkins for the standard garden, but for trellis gardens, they are fine.

SQUASH

This is a natural vining plant ideally suited to trellis gardening. Grown in conventional style, squash takes up large amounts of space, but on trellises it can be confined and still produce a bumper crop. The plants are exceptionally pretty with large handsome leaves and huge yellow flowers. Once started, squash requires buckets of water, and sun. Feed every other watering and thin plants to leave four or five stout stems for each 2-foot trellis. Pick vegetables early and often; they grow quickly and seem to double in size overnight. Big squash invariably have little taste. There are summer squash varieties and winter types. Bush squash also are available, but these are not as good for trellis gardens as the vining types.

Squash borers can sometimes be a problem with this vegetable so dust plants with *rotenone* in July or August.

TENDER LOVING CARE FOR VEGETABLES

To me, Tender Loving Care means keeping plants healthy. Even if you don't follow all the suggestions outlined here, the plants are likely to grow. The real test of TLC is to keep plants free from the insects and diseases that can quickly mow down a garden. Like people, plants catch diseases from other plants, and once insects get a foothold they keep moving from one plant to the next.

INSECTS

Most common insect pests are discernible by the human eye; it is just a question of spotting them. *Aphids* are tiny, oval, soft-bodied pests; *mealy bugs* are cottony masses hard to miss; and *scale* are hard-shelled insects that attach themselves to plants and somewhat resemble apple seeds. All these insects are easy to see and easy to get rid of if you catch them early. The one insect you will not be able to see that is liable to attack plants is *spider mite*. Its calling card if finely stippled leaves with silvery webs on the underside. Dry air is a common cause, so be forewarned.

In addition to the insects just mentioned, vegetables, depending upon the kind, will attract other unwanted visitors, although they may never appear if you keep a clean garden. Chewing insects of various kinds love leafy vegetables, so keep *rotenone* insecticide on hand. *Hornworms*, which are green worms about 4 inches long, and *cutworms*, may appear on tomatoes. Do not panic. Hand pick and destroy them, or use *Sevin* insecticide. Only one or two applications will be needed. *Cucumber beetles*, yellow critters with black stripes, are easily discouraged from squash and cucumbers by using a regular *rotenone* or *pyrethrum* insecticide. If you are growing beans, be on the alert for *bean leaf beetles* or *Mexican bean beetles*, which are about 1/4 inch long and copper colored with black spots. Use *Sevin* to control them.

Squash borers are brownish, flat-backed beetles. They are nefarious critters, and I hate them because I love squash. These insects can wipe out a good crop. If you see them, dust with *rotenone*, especially in July to August.

Last, but certainly not least, *snails* and *slugs* like vegetables almost as much as people do. Get snail and slug bait. I recommend *Corys* if you can find it. If not, try *Buggeta*. Sprinkle pellets on the soil.

Use these chemicals and all insecticides with care and only as directed on the package. It is especially important in any type of vegetable garden to observe caution on labels about discontinuing use a certain length of time before harvest.

DISEASES

Diseases rarely attack plants in a small garden. But, like insects that have favorite foods, diseases attack certain crops, too. For example, two serious tomato diseases, *verticillium* and *fusarium*, also known as *wilt*, may attack. You can identify wilt by a brown stain that appears in the woody tissues of the stem. Not much can be done once it occurs. Use steam of *formalin* to sterilize the diseased areas of soil where such plants have been growing. Many vegetable varieties are now disease-resistant; look for them because they are certainly worth the search.

BERRIES

Do not overlook berries for your garden, no matter how little space you have. Berries are essentially ramblers and, uncontrolled, take up space. But you can grow them on trellises and keep them within bounds and still have a great crop of fruit. Blueberries, blackberries, raspberries and strawberries are delicious fresh from the garden. Berry growing on a trellis or arbor is a challenging adventure. It takes time to prune and trim and train, but the results are worth it, not only for eating but also for looks. Rambling berries on arbors and trellises project a lovely

5'x5' POST GARDEN

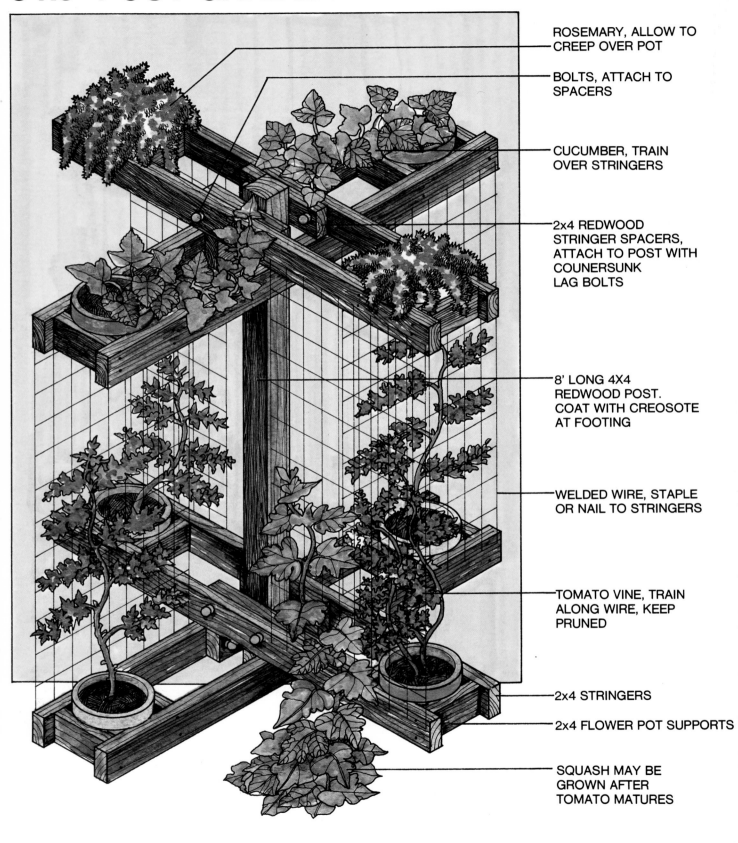

ROSEMARY, ALLOW TO CREEP OVER POT

BOLTS, ATTACH TO SPACERS

CUCUMBER, TRAIN OVER STRINGERS

2x4 REDWOOD STRINGER SPACERS, ATTACH TO POST WITH COUNERSUNK LAG BOLTS

8' LONG 4X4 REDWOOD POST. COAT WITH CREOSOTE AT FOOTING

WELDED WIRE, STAPLE OR NAIL TO STRINGERS

TOMATO VINE, TRAIN ALONG WIRE, KEEP PRUNED

2x4 STRINGERS

2x4 FLOWER POT SUPPORTS

SQUASH MAY BE GROWN AFTER TOMATO MATURES

5'x5' POST GARDEN

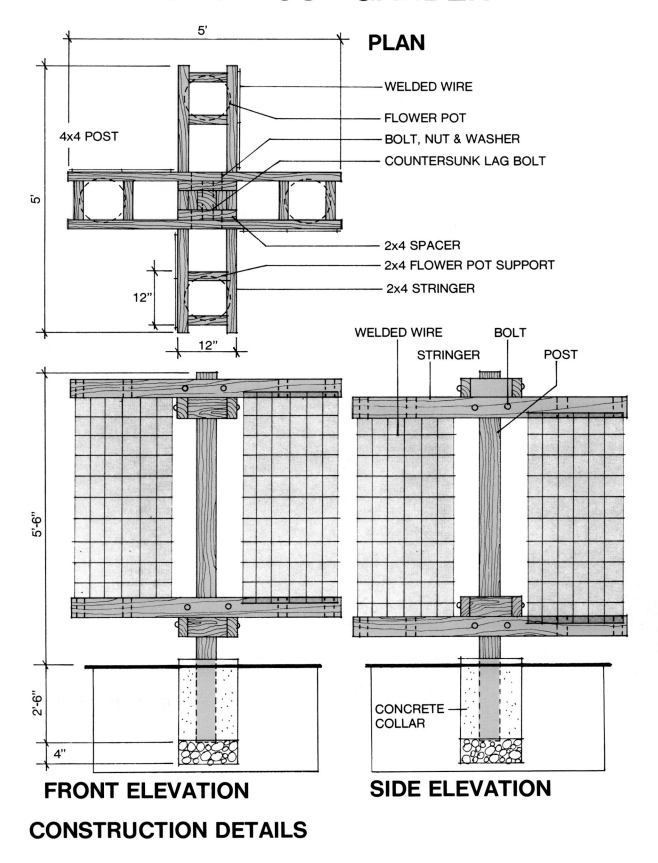

PLAN

5'

4x4 POST

5'

WELDED WIRE

FLOWER POT

BOLT, NUT & WASHER

COUNTERSUNK LAG BOLT

2x4 SPACER

2x4 FLOWER POT SUPPORT

2x4 STRINGER

12"

12"

WELDED WIRE · BOLT

STRINGER · POST

5'-6"

2'-6"

4"

CONCRETE
COLLAR

FRONT ELEVATION

SIDE ELEVATION

CONSTRUCTION DETAILS

old-fashioned charm that adds great warmth and character to the garden. Berries are best grown on wire trellises; wood trellises with enough open space can be used, too.

Select berry varieties that are suited for your geographical area. Blueberries are best in the cool northern areas; boysenberries and their relatives, blackberries and logan berries, are good in the humid south. You can grow strawberries in almost any part of the country. Care of different berries is covered in the specific fruits that follow.

RASPBERRIES

There are several kinds of raspberries—red, black, purple and yellow. Some are early producers, others yield crops in midseason and still others are late bearers. Select types best adapted to your area of the country; ask your nurseryman or your local agricultural agent. Buy one-year old stock, virus free.

Raspberries thrive on moisture and must have it to produce a bumper crop; they also need good drainage. Plant in early spring in northern climates; in fall in the south. Set red raspberries 2 to 3 inches deeper than they were growing in the nursery; black and purple types should be set 1 inch deeper than they were in their containers. After planting, cut back red raspberries to 8 to 12 inches. Black and purple raspberries are cut back to ground level. Plant berries 4 to 6 feet apart with trellis supports running the length of the planting. With berries, wire is the best type of trellis. You should use a span of 2 or 4 wires running parallel to the ground. Leave a 12- to 16-inch space between wires. Use post supports every 2 to 3 feet.

Red raspberries develop new shoots from both crown and root. Canes grow vigorously in summer, initiate flower buds in fall, rest over winter, then bear the following season. Once canes have borne fruit,

they die. But the cycle will be repeated as new shoots appear to develop fruiting canes.

Allow five to eight fruiting canes per mature plant.

BLACKBERRIES

Blackberries can be pests in the garden because they are so invasive. They are best grown in planter boxes. They also can grow rampant on trellises, or you can prune them to prevent disorder.

To keep blackberries from taking over, start them growing vertically on wire trellises. And since a well-grown blackberry can yield a host of berries in a season, you do not need many plants to assure good eating. Blackberries produce canes that will bear fruit the year after they sprout. When the canes die, new ones spring up to replace the old ones. An established plant can bear up to 10 years.

The blackberry grows best in mild climates. It is a shallow rooted plant that requires ample moisture, good drainage and protection from drying winds. Common blackberry varieties, including thornless ones, are hardy, semi-hardy or tender. Check

with your local nursery, or university extension and pick the one that grows best in your area. Plant in spring in the north and in fall or early winter in the south.

Before you plant, trim away long roots and cut back tops to about 6 inches. Dig deep holes, spread roots out fanwise, and fill in with drainage material and soil. Pack soil tightly around the collar of the plant. Leave 3 to 5 feet between the plants, depending on the variety. During the first spring and summer, keep suckers cut. As soon as young shoots are up 2 or 3 feet, snap off the tips so lateral growth will start to bear fruit the following year. Keep vines trained to the trellis using tie-ons or nylon string to keep them in place. The following spring, prune laterals to about 18 inches. As soon as new canes are up, select four or five of the strongest and let them grow on the trellis. Remove others at ground level. When new canes are about 30 inches tall, *tip* them by pruning off 1 inch from the tip so they will prepare to bear fruit for the following year. Blackberries will bear some fruit in the second year, but the bumper crop comes in the third year.

BLUEBERRIES

Blueberries like an acid soil, so if you grow them, be sure the soil has a pH of about 4.2 to 5.0. To prepare your soil, add peat moss or partially decayed oak leaves, or acid food in packages, to make it acidic. Do not add manure because it tends to make soil alkaline. Sandy loam, sulphur and sawdust also help. This is discussed in more detail in Chapter 8.

Blueberries are largely self-sterile, so you will need a few different varieties to make plants bear fruit. The 'Highbush' type does well in North Carolina, New Jersey, Massachusetts and Michigan, and grows to about 8 feet. The 'Lowbush' berry is a small plant that grows to 3 feet, and is fine for New England states. The 'Rabbiteye' is best for the southeastern United States and is a good plant because it adapts to many soil conditions.

Plant blueberries when they are dormant, either in spring or fall. Be sure trellises are on hand. Dig large holes for each plant, twice the size of the root ball. Set the plant high in the ground with the crown 2 inches above the soil level. Space plants 6 to 8 feet apart. Feed plants sparsely, if at all, because, if fed too much, blueberries will be all leaves and no fruit.

Do not fertilize when planting bushes; wait until plants are fully mature. Pinch off all blossoms the first year after planting. Unlike other berries, blueberries require little if any pruning. You can occasionally prune lightly, but bear in mind that you want tall, erect, strong canes. Keep them trained to the trellis structure. Prune just enough to encourage lateral or side shoots, which is where fruit is borne. Remove laterals after fruiting to make room for new shoots. After 5 or 6 years, cut away to the ground older branches that are no longer producing good laterals. Blueberries literally can bloom themselves to death; it is up to you to keep them within reason by judiciously pruning laterals.

STRAWBERRIES

Strawberries are such an amenable crop that even the rankest amateur can grow them. These plants, which can be cultivated in most parts of the United States, are perennials that live for several years. They blossom and bear fruit each season. The best crops are produced the first 2 years; after that, the yield is not great. Strawberries usually are called *everbearing*, but there are also early, *midseason* and *late bearers*. There are three types: *Summer Fruiting, Perpetual* or *Remontant*, and *Alpine*. They could just as well be described as large, medium and small, for those are the respective sizes of fruit borne by each.

Just a dozen plants will yield a harvest for the novice, sparse in the first year, but prolific in the second year. When you are ready to start your plants, build a trellis pyramid for them. It takes up little space and is attractive. Use three 3-foot trellises; tall supports are not necessary. Trim roots back to 3 or 5 inches, dig holes wide enough to accommodate the roots, and set the plants in place. Set plants so that crowns are at ground level. If plants are placed too deep in the hole, growth will be retarded. If they are too high, they will die. The plants need a rich moist soil and plenty of sun to do their best. The ideal soil is sandy loam, but strawberries prosper even in poor soil, if there is good drainage. In the north, start plants in spring; in the south, plant in fall. Summer Fruiting and Remontant varieties should be spaced about 18 inches apart. The smaller Alpine plants may be spaced a foot apart.

The strawberry plant is a member of the rose family and has lovely white scented blossoms that resemble wild roses. Leaves are produced on short woody stems. Train the

Opposite Page
Berries are easily grown on trellises.

3'x3' TRIPLE-DECKER GARDEN

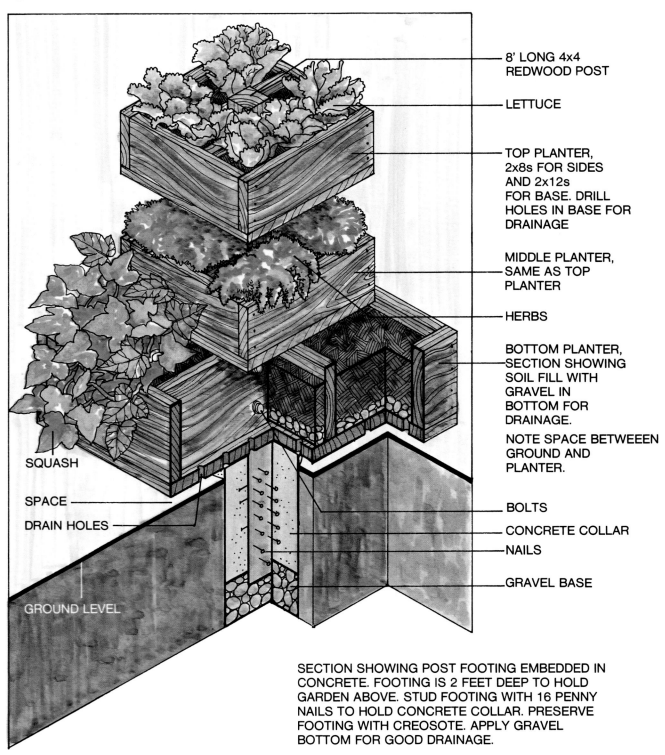

8' LONG 4x4 REDWOOD POST

LETTUCE

TOP PLANTER, 2x8s FOR SIDES AND 2x12s FOR BASE. DRILL HOLES IN BASE FOR DRAINAGE

MIDDLE PLANTER, SAME AS TOP PLANTER

HERBS

BOTTOM PLANTER, SECTION SHOWING SOIL FILL WITH GRAVEL IN BOTTOM FOR DRAINAGE.

NOTE SPACE BETWEEEN GROUND AND PLANTER.

BOLTS

CONCRETE COLLAR

NAILS

GRAVEL BASE

SQUASH

SPACE

DRAIN HOLES

GROUND LEVEL

SECTION SHOWING POST FOOTING EMBEDDED IN CONCRETE. FOOTING IS 2 FEET DEEP TO HOLD GARDEN ABOVE. STUD FOOTING WITH 16 PENNY NAILS TO HOLD CONCRETE COLLAR. PRESERVE FOOTING WITH CREOSOTE. APPLY GRAVEL BOTTOM FOR GOOD DRAINAGE.

3'x3' TRIPLE-DECKER GARDEN

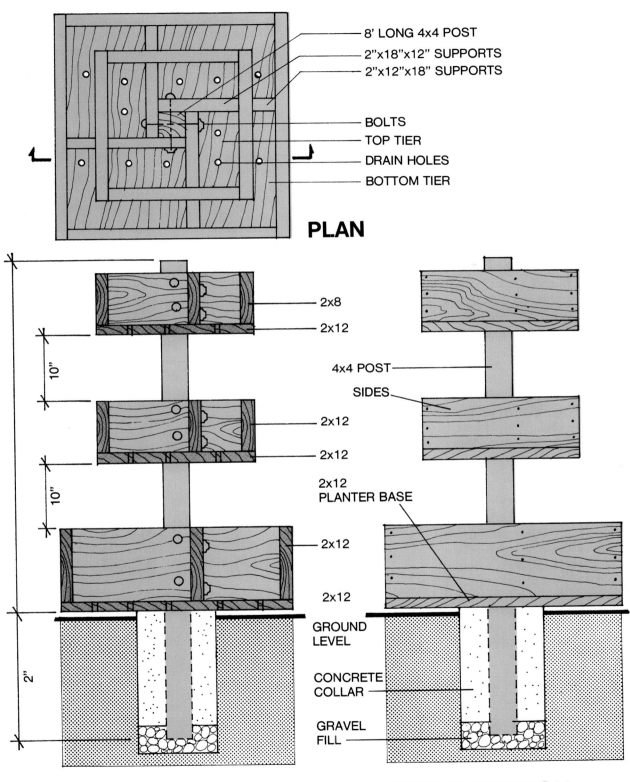

8' LONG 4x4 POST
2"x18"x12" SUPPORTS
2"x12"x18" SUPPORTS

BOLTS
TOP TIER
DRAIN HOLES
BOTTOM TIER

PLAN

2x8
2x12

4x4 POST
SIDES

2x12
2x12

2x12
PLANTER BASE

2x12

2x12

GROUND LEVEL

CONCRETE COLLAR

GRAVEL FILL

10"
10"
2"

SECTION

SIDE ELEVATION

CONSTRUCTION DETAILS

leaves to the trellis, securing them with tie-ons or string. Most gardeners pinch the first blossoms from strawberries to get a better yield. The strength of the plant will not be depleted by setting fruit too early, and the resultant crop will be heavy when the plant matures. I pinch off some, but not all, of the blossoms and have a fine crop of berries. Not every strawberry flower produces fruit; cross pollination by insects or wind is necessary.

FRUITS

Many people want to grow delicious fruits like apples and pears, but generally there is not enough space. What to do? Espalier the trees on trellises and have any or all of the fruit you want. For example, in a space of 20 feet, say, against a fence, you can grow four dwarf fruit trees.

Training plants—all kinds of plants—to specific patterns is not new, but it is certainly an overlooked part of gardening. Yet a well-groomed espalier against a trellis can be more attractive than a row of foundation plantings, and think of the space saved!

Espaliering is training a plant to grow against a flat surface. A plant grown to an espalier pattern is trimmed to a desired shape. Generally, the plant is tied to a trellis that is parallel to a flat surface, with 4 to 6 inches of air space behind the plant. In some cases, espaliers are applied directly to a wall.

If possible, buy an espalier that is already started at a nursery. It is much easier to train a tree or shrub that is already started than to initiate the pattern yourself. Do not be in a rush with espaliers; they take time to grow and cover an area, but once established, they are indeed handsome.

ESPALIER PATTERNS

Years ago there were rigid espalier patterns, but now the designs are personal choices. The formal patterns, although still seen, are not as popular as the informal or free-form espaliers. The formal patterns are quite symmetrical and include the following:
- **The Double Horizontal Cordon**—A center shoot about 20 inches high, with two horizontal branches in each direction.
- **The Vertical U Shape**—A vertical stem on each side of a central trunk. Double and triple U shapes also are seen.
- **The Palmette Verrier**—A handsome candelabra pattern.
- **The Palmette Oblique**—Branches trained in a fan shape.
- **The Horizontal T**—A multiple horizontal cordon with several horizontals on each side of a vertical trunk.
- **Belgian Espalier**—A diamond pattern.
- **Arcure**—A series of connecting arcs.

Informal espaliers are most natural and, to my eye, more pleasing for most properties. The patterns are casual or free-form. The informal espalier does not require as much trimming and training as the formal pattern, but creating an open and beautiful design still is the goal. Supports generally are not necessary; you can tie stems of plants to surfaces with special nails or copper wire.

Espalier fruit trees can be grown in containers or in the ground. Use a well-drained, rich soil and choose appropriate plants for the conditions you can give them. For example, use sun lovers against a south wall, shade lovers at a northern or western exposure. Do not fertilize espaliers; too much feeding will make it impossible to keep them trained to the desired shape.

GETTING STARTED WITH FRUIT TREES

Fruit trees bear at different times of the year. For example, there are apples for early season, midseason and late season—well into fall—so it is wise to select trees for the season you want. Just how long it will be before trees will bear is another consideration; apples and pears bear in 4 to 6 years; plums, cherries and peaches bear in about 4 years.

You should also think of size. There are standard-size fruit trees and dwarf ones that grow only a few feet tall. There are many varieties of apples, peaches and cherries. You should check with your local nurseryman about which do best in your area. Your trees must be hardy enough to stand the coldest winter and the hottest summer in your vicinity.

Many varieties of fruits, including the tree fruits, are self-sterile, which means that they will not set a crop unless other blossoming plants are nearby to furnish pollen. Some fruit trees are self-pollinating or fruiting and need no other tree. When you buy your fruit trees, ask about this. Fruit trees are beautiful just as decoration, but you want fruit to eat, too.

APPLES

Apples can be grown in every state except Florida. Apples are the hardiest of tree fruits. Apple trees tolerate a wide variety of climates; some will even tolerate $-20°F$ $(-29°C)$. The ideal climate for apples is somewhat cool, with plenty of sun and abundant rainfall. Choose the variety that is best suited for your climate. Varieties that thrive in northeastern states may not grow in the south.

Reasons for Low Yield—Apple trees sometimes kill themselves by bearing too much fruit. Trees should carry only as much fruit as they can support. So thin out fruit if you have the time. If the trees bear little or no fruit, the causes may be over production the previous year, a late frost that killed the flower buds, or lack of pollination because only one variety was planted.

Pick apples when they are firm.

Twist them from the tree; do not pull. If they do not come off easily with a slight turn of your wrist, they are not yet ready. If you pull off the fruit, the *spur*, the fruiting part of the branch, may come off, preventing further fruit production.

Insects that attack apples include aphids, leaf rollers, apple maggots and scale. Diseases include apple scab and blight. Remedies are available for each. Check with your nurseryman for advice.

CHERRIES

Cherries, sour or sweet, are an overlooked, but delightful crop. The sweet cherries—'Bing' and 'Queen Anne'—are delicious when eaten off the tree. Sour cherries are great for preserves, jams and pies. Sour cherries also are much hardier and easier to grow than sweet ones. Generally, cherries grow under the same climatic conditions as apples. Sour cherries bear in the fourth or fifth year; sweet ones bear a few years later.

Make sure the cherry trees you buy are *double bearing* or pollination will be difficult. Cherry trees require good light, so be sure they are pruned properly every year. Prune so that five or six limbs of your cherry tree become the main bearing limbs. Leave a single top growing straight up as a leader on the trellis, but trim other branches so they are shorter than the leader. Prune so there is plenty of open space and good vertical shape.

Cherry trees are not as prone to diseases and insects, other than tent caterpillars, as most trees. But they attract birds that will eat the cherries long before you even see them. Ugly netting is one solution, but the best thing to do is pray—and hope the birds arrive after the cherries develop or the cherries arrive before the birds find them. As a decoy, plant a mulberry tree; birds like mulberries even better than cherries.

PEACHES

Peaches are a genuine taste treat, but peach trees will try your patience. They will grow in almost all parts of the country, but they are temperamental, bearing heavily one year but not the next. Peaches need both cold—below 40°F (4°C)—and warmth. But some varieties are so cold sensitive, one cold snap can wipe them out. Yet without summer warmth, fruit is sparse. In spite of all their problems, peaches grown in your own small-space garden are worth every effort because they are indescribably delicious, and unlike any peach you can get at a market.

Generally, peach trees are self-pollinating, but it is wise to plant two or three trees. They will bear in about four years. Peaches need severe pruning when they are first planted because they do not take well to transplanting. By pruning the tops you encourage root development, providing the tree with a good start. Cut the *leader*, the center branch, slightly; cut all other branches to about 4 inches. Tie stems to trellises with tie-ons or nylon cord to pattern desired. Prune slightly every year; a severe pruning should be given only at the start.

PEARS

Pears need a good winter chill to be at their best and will grow in the same regions as apples and peaches. Pears flower earlier than apple trees, so frost may be a problem. Unlike cherries and apples, which need a good rich soil, pears will do fairly well even in a poor soil if there is good drainage. Use different varieties of pear trees to ensure pollination, although they are mostly self-pollinating. Pear trees need very little pruning, almost none, so do not worry about them.

At the start, tie branches to the trellis, cut away errant branches and leaves, and train to desired espalier pattern. Pears do exceptionally well as espalier subjects.

Special Gardens
Herbs & Roses
8

Opposite Page
Your herb garden does not have to be this formal, but it will produce the same delicious herbs for you. Photo by Max Eckert.

Below
One herb that will grow well in most areas is rosemary. It makes a handsome ground cover with its blue flowers, but is very attractive to bees.

Even in the small garden it is possible to have a special section of herbs, vegetables, or even roses. Indeed, the herb garden can be grown in a very small area and provide more than enough seasonings for an average family all summer. A compact method of raising vegetables is described in Chapter 7. A beautiful rose garden can—with clever design—be created on a diminutive scale.

Plan these gardens carefully; use every inch of available space. Although they may not be as grandiose as their larger counterparts, they offer great satisfaction to the homeowner.

HERB GARDENS

Herb gardens were once intricately patterned, but today's herb garden is much less formal. Often it can be put in place in a weekend. Some plan is necessary, but elaborate designs are not needed. Yet for all its simplicity, the herb garden can be an artful mixture of foliage textures and colors joining with flower form and gentle color.

The small herb garden close to the kitchen is, of course, a convenience. Or the garden can be used as

an accent away from the house; here, of course, a more formal design might be needed. But no matter where you put the garden, choose a sunny place. Herbs do not do well in shaded areas. The garden should be neat and weeded, with paths and some borders to set it off in the landscape. A good background, such as a wall, fence or even a hedge, helps too.

The garden design can take many shapes, such as a wagonwheel, butterfly or even a knot. It can include herbs for fragrance, flavor and medicinal uses. Herbs are divided into several groups, although there is some overlapping. Those grown for fragrance are known as *aromatic herbs. Culinary herbs* are used for seasoning food. *Medicinal herbs* have an infinite variety of uses. There is special charm in a herb garden, and it is a delight to be able to pick your own seasonings.

Planning and Planting—Select a well-drained site for the herb garden so that water will not stand around plant crowns. A place with a slight slope is good. Most herbs prefer a neutral or slightly alkaline soil. If your soil is acid, apply liberal amounts of limestone to the garden each spring. As I said before, be sure the site has plenty of sun. Eight hours daily is ideal. Most herbs require more than four hours each day.

To prepare the garden, stake out the area with string and stakes. Remove any debris, large stones and weeds. Work the soil until it is porous and crumbly. Dig down 12 to 18 inches and prepare the ground carefully so the plants will thrive. Do not attempt to plant in dry clay soil or the herbs will die.

Selecting Herbs—Hardy perennial herbs are bought as young plants. Annuals and biennials are started yearly from seed. Put perennials in the ground in spring, and, when frost danger is over, sow seed for the annuals and biennials. Sprinkle

HERBS FOR FRAGRANCE

Artemisia abrotanum
 Southernwood
Asperula odorata
 Sweet woodruff
Lavandula dentata
 French lavender
Lavandula spica
 English lavender
Lavendula vera
Lippia citriodora
 Lemon verbena
Mentha citrata
 Orange mint
Mentha crispa
 Curled mint
Mentha rotundifolia
 Apple mint
Monarda didyma
 Bergamot
Ocimum minimum
 Basil
Origanum
 Marjoram
Pelargonium crispum
 Citronella geranium
Pelargonium denticulatum
 Skeleton geranium
Pelargonium graveolens
 Rose geranium
Pelargonium limoneum
 Lemon geranium
Pelargonium mellissinum
 Balm geranium
Pelargonium odoratissimum
 Apple geranium
Rosmarinus officinalis
 Rosemary
Ruta graveolens
 Ruse
Sactolina chamaecyparissus
 Lavender cotton
Satureja hortensis
 Summer savory
Satureja montana
 Winter savory
Thymus, in variety
 Thyme

the seeds over prepared soil and then cover with a light layer of soil. Moisten thoroughly with a fine mist.

Germination of seed varies with the herb, so don't panic if some herbs take a long time to sprout. Keep the plants reasonably moist during this time. Most seeds should be planted in the spring, but herbs such as thyme, dill and parsley can be sown in summer too. Herbs should be cut just as the flowers are about to open. This is when the essential oils are most abundant.

ROSE GARDENS

Roses are popular flowers with a romance all their own. They have been with us for a very long time and continue to be admired and grown. A well-designed rose garden is indeed a stunning sight.

Planning and Planting—In planning this garden choose a place that has some air circulation, but is still protected from the wind. Try to select a neutral background so that the roses will be seen to their best advantage. Install brick or fieldstone paths to enhance the beauty of the garden, and decide upon a definite pattern for the beds.

Roses need a fertile, well-drained, slightly acid soil with a pH ranging from 5.5 to 6.5. Because rose roots are long, dig deeply, to about 20 inches when you prepare the bed. Take out an additional 3 to 6 inches and replace the soil with cinders or crushed stone to ensure good drainage. Roses will grow in a fairly clayey or sandy soil, but they will not thrive unless drainage is almost perfect and the soil is fertile.

For a good bloom, be sure the garden is in a sunny spot; roses need about 5 hours of sun daily. Some shade is beneficial in the afternoon.

The planting time depends upon your climate. In cold areas, early spring is best for setting out dormant bushes. In the mid-part of the country, early spring or late fall is suggested, and in all-year climates, roses can be planted from November to January. Be sure the crown of the plant is one or two inches below the soil surface. Pack soil firmly around the roots; avoid loose planting.

Roses need an evenly moist soil throughout the growing season, and do give them deep soakings rather than frequent light sprinklings. Don't give them overhead watering. This can cause black spots to form on the foliage.

The amount of winter protection depends on the weather in your locality and the type of rose. Check in your area for this information.

Feeding—In the first season of growth, feeding may not be necessary if the original planting was done with care. In the second year start a fertilization program. Roses

are heavy feeders. Give them at least two or three feedings a year: the first in spring soon after pruning, the second in June before bloom, and the third in summer. I use a 5-10-5 fertilizer for roses, but check in your area to see what is being used with most success. Be sure the soil is moist when applying fertilizer and work it into the soil around

plants with a rake.

Planting distances depend upon the type of rose. For hybrid and tea roses, a distance of 18 to 24 inches apart is fine. Floribundas and grandifloras need more space: about 18 to 36 inches between each plant. Trim the roses before you plant them, and remove broken or injured roots. As mentioned, plant roses

Opposite Page, Top
Climbing roses will completely cover a fence or wall, giving rich color and abundant blossoms.

Opposite Page, Bottom
Low-growing roses can be used as edges or borders.

deep and place them in position, so that the crown (point of union between the stock and scion) is between one and two inches below the surface of the soil. In mild climates the bud union should be just above the surface of the soil. After planting, pack the soil firmly around the roots and keep the roses well watered the first few weeks until they are established.

Pruning—Roses need pruning to produce strong roots and shoots; without proper cutting they get leggy and dense. Pruning depends upon the type of rose and the locality, but there are some general rules to remember. Remove dead or weak wood and maintain the desired height. Use sharp pruning shears and make a slant cut above a vigorous bud. To guard against fungi, treat the ends of cut stems with a fungicide. In spring before growth starts, prune plants just above a node (bud). Cut in a slanting direction and leave three to five buds on each stem. Only light pruning is needed for rambler roses that bloom on old wood. Roses that bloom on new wood from the base of the plant need pruning after flowering.

Selecting Plants—Bare-root plants are most often selected by gardeners. These are dormant and ready to start a new cycle of growth when you get them. If you cannot plant them immediately, keep them cool and be sure the roots are kept moist. Never allow rose roots to become dry before they are planted. Put them in water until you get the plants in the ground.

Packaged roses are often available. If they have been stored in a cool place, they are satisfactory. If the branches look dry and shriveled, chances are they have been kept in a hot location, so don't buy them.

Container-grown roses are already started for you. They cost more than dormant ones, but for beginners these are the best buy.

In cold regions, plants should be protected for the winter. Place mounds of soil about ten inches high around them. Do not scoop the soil from around the plant; rather, bring in fresh soil. Remove the covering gradually in spring when growth starts.

Because there are so many roses available, first decide what kind you want. The following discussion should help you, but it lists only a few varieties. There are many more available.

Good display and cutting roses include *hybrid teas, floribundas* and *grandifloras*. The hybrid teas have a sturdy growing habit and are hardy in the north if given suitable winter protection. They give generous bloom from June to September. Some varieties grow over 3 feet tall. Others are low growers. There is a wide range of color and form.

Floribunda varieties vary greatly in size. Some are almost dwarf and others grow to 6 feet. Flower form is single to semidouble in a wide range of colors. These plants are very floriferous and less demanding than most roses.

Grandifloras are very vigorous, free-blooming and easy to grow. The flowers appear in clusters and last very long.

Edging roses are dwarf, generally of the *polyantha* group. They are very hardy and give generous blooms throughout the season.

Hedge roses are quick growing, tall and busy, and they require very little care.

Old-fashioned roses generally have single flowers and include old favorites, such as the provence rose and the damask rose.

Climbing roses can be trained to supports. Some are rampant, but others are more restrained in growth. Some have a peak season of bloom while others flower intermittently throughout the season. A few varieties are very hardy, but others are suitable only for mild climates.

Special Features 9

Opposite Page
Primroses around this beautiful pool create a quiet, timeless place.

SPECIAL TOUCHES

Once your design is established and your plants selected, it is time to think of those small additions that will make your small space truly special. Lighting and a spa or pool can turn an outdoor space into an extra room that you will use over and over.

LIGHTING

A garden at night—properly lighted—can be a dramatic place. And today, with low-voltage systems, lighting is easy to install and within the means of most home-owners.

A lovely small garden seems to demand lighting. By day it is beautiful, but at night it can be transformed completely by dramatic lighting. Trees and shrubs, pools and fountains, patios and paths take on new dimension when properly illuminated. Water gardens sparkle and garden ornaments—statues or figures—seem to come alive. Lighting is necessary not only for beauty but for safety too.

Many principles are involved in the art of landscape lighting, so if your grounds are large, it might be wise to seek professional help. But for the homeowner with average size property, here are some helpful hints.

Silhouette Lighting—This is light coming from above to create halos below, or light coming from below to silhouette the plants. The light source is directed at a wall, fence or shrubbery from behind the object, with very little brightness at the front.

Etched Lighting—This type of lighting is used to emphasize the texture of tree bark, masonry walls or architectural objects. The light source is placed at a distance of 4 to 10 inches and aimed parallel to the surface of the object.

Contour Lighting—This type of lighting is used for creating depth and three-dimensional character in a subject. Light is aimed at an object from several directions, with more light coming from one side than from the other.

Colored Lighting—The purpose of colored lighting is to emphasize the color of plants. This is achieved with the same color light as the object illuminated.

Occasionally, light itself becomes the object to be seen, adding little illumination. It can be used as a substitute for plants to fill spaces with shadow and light rather than with leaf and branch.

The placement of fixtures is vital in outdoor lighting. Whenever possible, they should be concealed from view. Do not use too many lights, but station them in the right places. Paths and walks should be illuminated for safety, and patios and terraces for nighttime use. Certain trees and shrubs, although not all of them, deserve a bright spot focused on them.

Select a focal point—a branching tree or a piece of statuary—and start there. Make the light brighter in this area than in other places. The best time to arrange lights is at night by trial and error. A few inches one way or another makes a big difference.

Create an interplay of light and shadow. Keep the illumination at different intensity levels throughout the garden. Do not light a subject head-on; that will wash away details. Strive for a soft, diffused effect to bring out textures, shadows and contours. Place fixtures on two sides of an object rather than on one side. Use walls and fences as reflecting surfaces. Most of all, follow this basic rule in all lighting: Do not aim fixtures at your neighbors' property.

TYPE OF LIGHTING

Low-voltage lighting systems are now a part of the evening scene, and conventional 120-volt lighting is now more sophisticated. It is no longer necessary to protect wires in rigid conduits. New chemically coated wire can be buried directly in the ground. However, conventional lighting entails more work and time than installing low-voltage systems. Trenches at least 18 inches deep still must be dug to bury wires. Outlet boxes are necessary, and generally, trench cable must be grounded. These are jobs for a qualified electrician, and often require approval by local building inspectors before they can be used.

Low-voltage systems are an easier way to light the landscape and a far safer one. Even if you accidentally cut a cable with a spade, there will be a spark but no shock. Or, if you poke your finger inside a fixture, there is little danger of shock. Also, building codes usually do not require an inspection. Be forewarned, however, that for an effective lighting plan, both kinds of systems are usually needed.

The secret of the low-voltage system is a simple transformer that attaches to the side of the house and plugs into any outdoor outlet. This unit reduces the normal 120-volt house system to 12 volts. Unlike the cables for the 120-volt system that must be deeply buried in the ground, low-voltage cables can be set 1 inch below the soil. Just wedge the earth apart with a spade, put the cables in place, and tamp down the soil with your shoe.

The systems come in kits with a transformer and either 4, 6 or 8 lights, and about 100 feet of cable. Most kits have resealing cable; you can clip on fixtures to the cable at any point.

Low-voltage lighting is soft and subdued. It is excellent for decorative effects along flower beds, walks and paths, and steps. But for additional light for large areas, such as lawns and patios, you may need the standard 120-volt system.

Sometimes several kits are necessary to light all outdoor areas adequately. Therefore, set apart each area—garden, patio, pool, walks and steps—and install a separate system for each place. This makes it easy to shut off light in areas you do not want to use.

Decide exactly where you want light before you start buying fixtures. It is a good idea to make a rough plan on paper. Decide which area is most important in your scheme of living. Perhaps a mass of light for the patio, with subdued illumination for other areas, is the best answer to your outdoor-living scheme.

BULBS AND FIXTURES

The mainstay for outdoor lighting is the PAR lamp. It is a sealed unit generally in the shape of a mushroom. It is not affected by water, snow, ice or fluctuating temperatures. Some PAR lamps are used for floodlighting an area while others are for spotlighting a single object. They are available in different wattages: 75, 100 and 150. Higher intensities also are available for landscapes; these include 200-, 300- and 500-watt lamps. Install all lamps in fixtures with waterproof sockets.

The common household bulb can be used outdoors too. Bulbs of 15 watts or 25 watts used for wall brackets and path fixtures do not need protection from weather, but bulbs with higher wattages do. Where lines of light are needed, say,

along a flower bed or a path, fluorescent lamps from 14 to 40 watts can be used in weatherproof sockets. For outdoors, *cool white* or *daylight* types are the best. Colored bulbs are available too. Avoid strong colors such as red and green which will create a carnival effect. Pink, blue-white, yellow and amber are better choices.

Fixtures come in a variety of designs: some are very ornamental and simulate flowers or leaves, rocks or frogs. The standard fixture is a bullet reflector type. Canopy fixtures, cones and mushroom shaped fixtures, as well as louvered kinds also are available at suppliers. Some are portable, mounted on metal spikes that stick into the ground, while others are for permanent installation on a tree or post. Recessed units and flush-mounted fixtures are available for areas where there is little natural shielding.

Underwater fixtures come in the same mushroom shape as PAR fixtures or as separate housings.

POOLS AND FOUNTAINS

A small pool or fountain in a garden area greatly enhances the scene and creates a peaceful setting. Even in a limited garden area you can have a spot for water. If you like the idea of soaking in a hot tub, these units also are suitable for the small garden.

GARDEN PONDS AND POOLS

Small pools to about 24 inches in diameter have their limits, but they are pretty. Use them for what they are—a charming picture placed near a path or a patio where they can be seen. Embellish them with ground cover plants at the edges, or seasonal plants in the background.

Small stone, metal or rigid plastic bowls are available at most nurseries. Generally, these are shallow receptacles about 8-inches deep, with a maximum 24-inch diameter. They can be placed below grade so that the water level is even with the soil,

Upper Left
Small water garden gives a unique character to this house. Photo courtesy of California Redwood Association.

Upper Right
More elaborate hot tub is protected from the weather.

Left
A wooden hot tub on a wooden deck has become a symbol of relaxation.

Lower Right
Small garden pond is perfectly lit for nighttime pleasure.

or they can fit into a concave mound of soil for a raised pool. These small pools are attractive as a spot of water in the landscape. They are inexpensive and usually do not require plumbing connections. They can be filled and emptied with a garden hose.

Salvaged pool forms for small amounts of water are in the same category as the bowls mentioned above. These include photographers' darkroom trays, surplus plastic bubble domes, laundry tubs, wine barrels or anything your imagination can dream up.

Choose a site for the pool that is a low spot in the small garden— it will seem natural in this position. Before doing any planting, cover the edges of the pool with flat rocks or stones and fill in between with soil.

ONE-PIECE-MOLDED POOLS

These are generally irregular in shape, and fall into the category of informal or natural pools. The largest I have seen holds about 200 gallons of water and is approximately 8 by 6 feet by 18 inches deep; the smallest is about 5 feet in diameter and holds about 50 gallons of water 7 inches deep. They are all one-piece-molded construction of tough resin-bonded fiberglass and look like over-sized bathtubs.

The small pool in my garden was put in years ago before rigid plastics were available, but from what I am told by gardeners, the new molded containers are quite satisfactory, and they are much easier to put in place. Deep digging is not necessary, for the pool can be sunk in a depression in the ground half its depth. The excavated soil is then packed around the sides. When preparing the excavation for the resin pools, remove all sharp-pointed stones, for they may penetrate the base and cause damage.

FOUNTAINS AND WATERFALLS

The fountain or waterfall adds still another element to the landscape—the sound of water in motion. Today, fountains are enjoying a rebirth. The simplest kind is a single stream rising in a jet from the center. There are also spray-type, splash-type and drip fountains, and dozens of manufactured heads that put water in motion in every shape—from a column to a lacelike spray.

Power is needed to keep the water moving. This is provided by a recirculating pump which usually is available at nurseries. They vary in power, capacity and price. Some need to be immersed in water; others are located above the water line. Read the directions carefully. If necessary, consult the manufacturer or hire someone to put the unit into operation for you. In any case, select a pump that delivers more water than you originally estimated, Pump capacities can sometimes be misleading. Be sure to buy fittings that are the same diameter as those on the pump.

HOT TUBS AND SPAS

The wooden hot tub is a recent innovation and is appearing more and more in gardens. It is attractive, offers a pleasant way for family or friends to relax and creates a tranquil scene when surrounded with plants. Tubs or spas require little space and are easy to tuck away in a secluded corner. Add an overhead trellis and a few hanging plants and you can have complete privacy.

Tubs are purchased from manufacturers who supply all the pieces. There are dozens of styles. As with a fountain, the hot tub requires suitable hardware and fittings. Installation is best done by a professional.

Spas are usually single-piece fiberglass pools with systems for heating, filtering and moving water attached. Many people find the action of warm water flowing around them soothing and relaxing. Again, installation is best left to professionals.

PIVOTING SCREEN

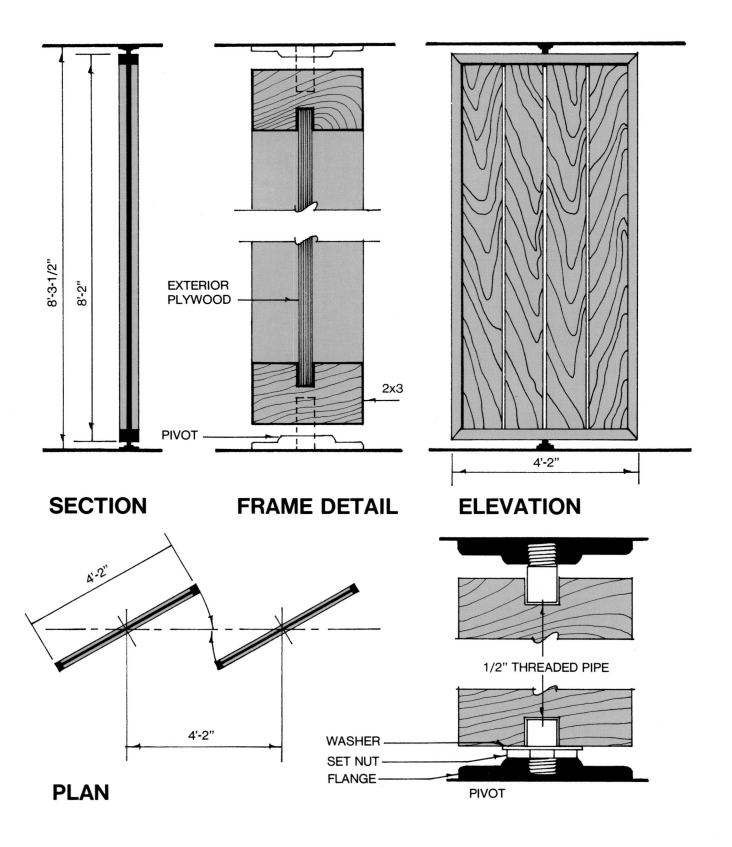

SECTION

8'-3-1/2"

8'-2"

FRAME DETAIL

EXTERIOR PLYWOOD

2x3

PIVOT

ELEVATION

4'-2"

PLAN

4'-2"

4'-2"

1/2" THREADED PIPE

WASHER
SET NUT
FLANGE

PIVOT

SCREENS

Sun and wind usually are severe problems for city gardners. Sun can be handled by using shade screens, canopies and so forth. Use tall plants in containers placed on the sides to break the wind and also screen you from neighbors. Use smaller plants and flowers for color and drama.

A roof or overhang or screen provides protection from weather and adds further dimension to a small garden. Construction takes a little know-how but is not beyond the average person's capabilities. The overhang or screen may be wood, plastic or canvas.

Upper
These screens move up with the terraces to insure privacy and provide a background for plants. Photo courtesy of Western Wood Products Association.

Lower
This screen serves several purposes at once. It provides a shield against noise and vision from the road outside; it shades the windows behind it; and it serves as a frame for an informal espalier. Photo courtesy of Western Wood Products Association.

Indoor Gardens
10

Live plants indoors can add beauty and color to any room, whether you live in a tiny apartment or a house. Windows are usually selected for indoor plants. This is fine but don't forget locations such as small alcoves, corners and other unused places where, with thought and imagination, you can create a garden indoors.

WINDOW GARDENS

The window garden as a decorative element serves several purposes. It brings fresh green into the room and provides a cheerful atmosphere. It can also act as drapery to give you privacy.

There is a wide array of plants to use for windows (where there is generally good light). However, most sills cannot accommodate any plant in a container more then 8 inches in diameter, even with shelving.

You can set your plants on a window sill, but there is always a danger of knocking them off their narrow perch. A better way is to install shelves. Attractive shelves for windows are now available in kits. They attach to the window frame with screws. Three shelves can give you space for as many as 30 plants. You can also make your own shelf arrangements.

Pole shelves are another answer.

The poles, called *suspension poles,* attach to ceilings and floors without hardware. Heavy springs hold them in place. Trays are hung between the poles and these hold the plants. This vertical garden can accommodate as many as 15 plants and is available through mail-order ads in garden magazines.

Setting Up Your Display—Too many plants make the window garden a jungle and prevent light from entering the room. Too few plants look sparse and do not provide sufficient eye appeal. Group large plants on the bottom shelves or the sill. Place the smaller ones on upper shelves. Always be sure to allow growing space for your plants.

Too often window plants look unkempt, with leaves pushing against the glass. Thus select plants that are upright growers or low bushy ones rather than branching and sprawling types.

Also select your containers with care. Too many different pots create a jumbled effect that can ruin the beauty of the window garden. Standard terra-cotta pots are a wise choice. They look good in almost any surrounding, come in many sizes, and let moisture evaporate slowly through their walls. This is a big plus for many plants.

PLANTS FOR WINDOW GARDENS

Aglaonema commutatum
    Chinese evergreen,
    Spotted evergreen
Alocasia watsoniana
Begonia erthrophylla
    Beefsteak begonia
Begonia paulensis
Coleus in variety
Dieffenbachia amoena
    Dumb cane,
    Mother-In-Law Plant

Dieffenbachia bowmannii
Dieffenbachia hoffmannii
Dracaena sanderiana
Haemanthus coccineus
    Blood lily
Hoffmannia roezlii
Maranta leuconeura kerchoveana
    Prayer plant
Philodendron andreanum
Philodendron pertusum
    Swiss cheese plant
Philodendron verrucosum
Sansevieria trifasciata
    Snake plant

Upper Left
Plant stands are great space savers. Hanging plants further enhance this window.

Upper Right
Grouping various-sized plants at different heights can create a handsome scene. This garden is only 6 feet wide.

Lower Left
This large window gives enough light for a tall dizygotheca, and smaller calceolaria and cineraria. Orchids on shelves and hanging ivy geranium complete the scene.

Lower Center
Grouping large plants turned this difficult area into a beautiful scene.

Lower Right
Even a narrow stairway can be special.

PLANTS FOR PEDESTALS

Aglaonema commutatum
   Chinese evergreen
Aspidistra elatior
   Cast-iron plant
Beaucarnea recurvata
   Ponytail plant
Begonia imperialis
   'Otto Forster'
Begonia luxurians
Begonia 'Ricky Minter'
Blechnum brasiliense
Codiaeum
   Croton

Crassula argentea
   Jade tree
Dracaena sanderana
   Belgian evergreen
Echinocactus grusonii
   Golden barrel cactus
Euphorbia grandicornis
Neoregelia carolinae
Nephrolepis exaltata
   Many varieties, Boston fern
Philodendron panduriforme
Philodendron wendlandii
Woodwardia orientalis
   Chain fern

Decorative containers can also be used, such as a group of Chinese jardinieres. Attractive glazed containers and handsome porcelain cones are also available, but don't plant directly in these. Instead, use a standard clay pot and slip it into the decorative ones. This will be better for the plant and protect the decorative pot from water damage.

PEDESTALS

The advantage of the pedestal is that it elevates the plant, putting it on display. And the pedestal and plant can be moved. If you do not like them in one area, try them in another place. Also, the pedestal-plant combination saves buying more expensive tree-type plants. Yet they can serve the same purpose and provide vertical accent.

Pedestal plants come in 12- to 16-inch containers. Use compact growers or semitrailing plants. Branching plants will obstruct traffic. Good choices include many fine begonias, cacti and succulents, and lovely ferns.

Keep plants well groomed because they are always on display.

FLOOR PLANTS

These large plants can serve several purposes in a room. They

Combining pots, containers and hanging baskets give this dining area an intimate, private feeling.

FLOOR PLANTS

Agave americana 'marginata'
   Century plant
Araucaria excelsa
   Norfolk pine
Caryota mitis
   Fishtail palm
Cereus peruvianus
Chamaedorea elegans
   Parlor palm
Chamaredorea erumpens
   Bamboo palm
Chrysalidocarpus lutescens
   Butterfly palm
Citrus, many kinds
Clusia rosea
Cocos weddelleiana
Cyads, many species
Dieffenbachia exotica
Dracaena fragrans massangeana
   Corn plant
Dracaena marginata
Ficus benjamina
Ficus carica
   Common fig
Ficus lyrata
   Fiddleleaf fig

Howea forsterana
   Kentia palm
Lemairocereus marginatus
Lemairocereus thurberi
Lophocereus schottii
Pandanus veitchii
   Screw pine
Philodendron bipinnatifidum
Philodendron selloum
   Fingerleaf philodendron
Philodendron squamiferum
Phoenix roebelenii
   Miniature date palm
Podocarpus macrophyllus
Podocarpus nagi
Polyscias fruticosa
   Ming tree
Rhapis excelsa
   Lady palm
Schefflera actinophylla (Brassaia)
   Umbrella tree
Trichocereus spachianus
Veitchia merrillii
Vriesea fenestralis
Yucca aloifolia
   Spanish dagger

are large design elements, and, whether used in a corner or against a window or wall, they make impressive statements. A vertical plant like *Araucaria excelsa*, the Norfolk Island pine, is handsome in a corner. Palms with canopies of green fronds are also good floor plants, but be wary. Of the many palms, only a few are symmetrical and suitable for corners. And do not overlook flowering plants like camellias, large bromeliads, or even tall orchids. If the floor plant you select is not as tall as it appeared in the store and does not fill the desired area, put it on a plant pedestal.

Pastel walls are an excellent background for floor plants, making them dramatic showpieces. Every leaf is prominent, and the trunks and stems are beautifully silhouetted. A wall provides space for branching or "weeping" plants, and

the plant looks like sculpture. For stark beauty, try a cactus.

When placing plants against walls, never crowd them. Allow some space behind them. If plants are against walls with no windows, you will need to supply artificial light. Be sure to plan ahead for ceiling track and fixtures to accommodate lights. No plant will live long without some source of light.

Floor plants are usually in 20-inch diameter pots. Choose suitable containers in keeping with the character of the room.

Other good locations for taller plants are the foot of an open stairway or a stairwell. The plants serve two purposes: decoration for the space as well as handsome viewing from the stairs.

HALLS & ENTRYWAYS

Your entrance hall is where

people get their first impression of your home. Many times these areas have little or no natural light, so choosing plants that will tolerate low light levels is the key to success. If the space is large enough, try a plant on a pedestal. For tables, shelves and benches, concentrate on plants that can tolerate shady situations, such as *cissus* and *sansevieria*.

If there is no room for furniture in the hall or entryway, a plant may be your only way of providing some decoration. Use tall vertical specimens that do not take up too much space. Try a leafy *philodendron* or a tall *dizygotheca*, false aralia.

In halls without any natural light you might want to use a decorator's trick: Rotate plants between the living room and hall. This is easy if pots are on casters. You simply roll them to a new location.

Above all, do not forget cascading

plants for halls and entryways. They are impressive on tall tables or shelves where pendant leaves can cover straight lines or furniture hardware. Use appropriate mats and saucers so water does not stain furniture tops.

Finally, do not forget the appeal of a small bouquet of fresh flowers in hall areas. This is a fine way to say welcome to guests.

BEDROOMS

Plants do more than make a bedroom look nice; they impart a soft, relaxing character to the room. Graceful palms or ferns on tables or the floor are airy and appealing. They can make going to bed calming and waking up cheerful.

In the past, small plants were used on dressers or chests of drawers. Today's bedroom is designed more for living than just sleeping, so let your imagination go. If you are an avid gardener, this is the place to have many plants, because it is your private place. Try a pair of arching palms to grace a headboard.

Many bedrooms are divided into areas for sleeping, dressing and sitting. Plants can be used as dividers or screens to provide a sense of privacy. Baskets of plants arranged in line can form a column of green that acts as a screen.

Keep the watering can in the nearby bathroom so you will not forget to water plants.

BATHROOMS

The bathroom is often overlooked when considering plants, and yet, ironically, here is where many plants grow best. Humidity from your daily shower and the warmth of the bathroom are both conductive to making plants grow well. And plants distract from the sterile fixtures of the bathroom. Also, frosted glass in bathroom windows is an advantage for plant growth because it provides diffused light, not too bright, not too dark. This is exactly what most plants prefer.

Floor plants are usually too large for the limited space of a bathroom, but baskets of ferns and hanging plants on wall brackets can work well. There are many plants that will prosper in the bathroom: *fittonias, marantas, anthuriums* and even orchids! On vanities, shelves, or in hanging baskets, there are innumberable places for small- to medium-sized pot plants. Use distinct pots to complement the decor and try all kinds of plants. You will be surprised at how well they will grow.

If your bathroom has no windows, try some plants under fluorescent lights on a shelf or table, or use ceiling spotlights for convenience. Placing plants adjacent to mirrors will create a double reflection so two plants appear as four.

If the shower area is light and spacious, consider a tropical floating garden with plants in ornamental containers. This is highly effective. Do not let the bathroom be bare. Try to incorporate some plants into its design.

KITCHENS

If you need a personal touch in the kitchen, plants are the answer. Furthermore, because you spend a great deal of time in the kitchen, you will want cheerful, colorful plants to brighten gray days. No matter how small the kitchen is, there are herbs, flowering plants, and even creepers and mosses that can thrive and enliven the room. You can grow basil, chives, rosemary, sage and thyme in small pots at kitchen windows. There are dozens of medium-sized plants that will also prosper at windows, including *pileas, peperomias, marantas, ruellias* and *syngoniums*. Floor plants may be too large for the average kitchen, but if there is some space, try a small rhapis palm, a cycad or even some trailing begonias.

Shelves, cabinet tops and window sills are all prime spots for kitchen

Opposite Page, Left
All it took was a pair of African violets and some grape ivy to make this small nook verdant. Consider the setting before placing too many plants in one space.

Opposite Page, Right
Most plants will thrive in the moisture and diffused light of a bathroom. Here a 4-foot square planter holds pots. Artificial light comes from overhead. Photo by Hedrick Blessing.

plants. Such popular flowering plants as African violets, geraniums and miniature begonias grow luxuriantly because most kitchens have higher humidity than other rooms in the home. Cooking and running water add moisture to the air.

FURNITURE FOR PLANTS

Although large floor plants are fine for many places in the home, you may also want a number of small or medium-sized plants. Stands to hold them are made of wood, metal, glass shelving, or wrought-iron. A small painted ladder can also serve as a display area.

You can also use Plexiglas shelving to hold a few plants as a room accent. These are generally contemporary in design, and the green accent of plants are just right for contrast. Use three or four plants spaced according to how many shelves there are, rather than just one or two plants. Place the plants to either the front or the rear but not in the center, because there they invariably seem out of proportion to the total shelf unit. Wooden shelf units are also available, but these are bulky, and even plants on saucers will leave water stains on wood. Glass or Plexiglas shelves allow light to reach all plants, but wood may block light.

There are wrought-iron stands available that look like small spiral staircases. The shelves are adjustable, each holding one plant. Wooden pedestals come in various shapes and sizes, and in various styles, antique or modern, Greek or Chinese. Of course they also hold only one plant.

A WINDOW GREENHOUSE

When you add a window greenhouse to your home, you bring the outdoors indoors. You do not have to worry about whether there are trees and shrubs outside or gray concrete surrounding you. You can provide your own natural scene. In this space you can grow plants all

Upper
Kitchen windows are ideal for plants.

Lower
Wrought iron stand provides handsome decoration. White containers add a sense of uniformity.

year because of the conditions maintained by the greenhouse.

What you can grow depends on space; there is no other limitation. You can grow orchids, bromeliads, vegetables, herbs, even a few annuals and perennials. The kinds of plants are not a problem, but space will be. When planning your window greenhouse, take this factor into consideration.

You may want to build your own window greenhouse, or you may want to buy a prefabricated one. In either case, building a greenhouse is not difficult. Prefabricated greenhouses accommodate almost any type or size of window opening.

Practical Considerations—If you own your home, there is no problem about attaching a greenhouse to a window. However, in a rented apartment you should get permission from the owner. Usually a landlord will not object to the greenhouse because it will improve the property's appearance. And today even the most hardened superintendents have their own collection of greenery, so they are receptive to the idea of tenants having gardens.

If you build your own unit, or have it built, consider the materials available. Is metal better than wood, or is wood the answer? To many people wood is the ideal choice because it looks natural and gives a unified impression that never clashes with a building. On the other hand, aluminum is rustproof and sleek in appearance. But metal is harder to work with than wood.

You can buy wood molding at lumber dealers or metal channels at supply yards. The best wood for your greenhouse is redwood because it resists weathering. The best metal is aluminum because it resists rust. The wooden window greenhouse will be about 25 percent less expensive to make than a metal unit. The average wooden greenhouse for a 24 by 30-inch opening should not cost more than $100. Homemade metal units run about $125.

If you do not have the time to make your own greenhouse or are not handy with tools, get a prefabricated unit. Prefab greenhouses come knocked down with all pieces included. If you buy a prefab greenhouse, ask if it can be installed from the outside, and always determine whether you must remove the window frame or if you can leave it in place. With most prefab models, the window frame can stay in place, but some units are designed so that it must be removed.

The easiest installation of any window greenhouse is at ground level because you can work on the outside without ladders. If you live in a high-rise apartment building, the unit must be assembled from the inside, which is possible with most, but not all, greenhouse models.

Where to Put It—The greenhouse should be set in a south, east or west window, where there is ample light. If other buildings interfere with the sunlight or the greenhouse must occupy a north window, there are numerous plants that can grow in shady places.

Perhaps the most logical place is the kitchen. People spend a good deal of time there, and a lovely green scene boosts the spirits early in the morning. Of course watering plants in the kitchen is convenient. The disadvantage in placing the greenhouse in the kitchen is that most kitchens have only one window. Fresh air would be blocked when the window greenhouse is in place. If this is not objectionable, then the kitchen should be the first choice.

The second-best location for a window greenhouse is the bathroom. Plants look good in bathrooms, softening the sometimes harsh lines or sterile colors. And again, water is only an arm's length away.

A living or dining room does not work well with a greenhouse unless the unit is custom designed to look like part of the building rather than a tacked-on afterthought. If the greenhouse is designed to coordinate with the rest of the architecture, it can be very handsome. You can create a marriage of indoors and outdoors by putting some potted plants on the floor or at the sides of the window to create balance and proportion.

Cellars or basements should not be ignored. These areas are fine places for greeneries. A window greenhouse can add beauty to a

sterile basement and create a perfect retreat, a hidden place to work with plants.

WHAT YOU CAN GROW

Undoubtedly you will want to grow such houseplants as *philodendrons* and *dieffenbachias,* but other beautiful plants, such as orchids, do splendidly in a window greenhouse.

Begonias will thrive, especially the angel-wings with their bright pink and white flowers. The smaller gesneriads, such as African violets and *episcias,* are excellent choices for the greenhouse, and a number of other flowering plants like *streptocarpus* and *heterocentron* are ideal. The thousands of miniature varieties are also perfect candidates for greenhouse cultivation.

You can also grow vegetables like eggplant, tomatoes, cucumbers and peppers. Almost any dwarf vegetable variety will work well, but vining squash, peas, and beans quickly outgrow the space. Many herbs do well in a greenhouse too.

BASIC INDOOR PLANTS

The following plants are
easy to care for and hardy.
They will thrive in the exposure
listed, but most can do well
in other exposures as well.

South or East Window
Vegetables
  Carrots
  Cucumbers, midget varieties
  Green peppers, midget
   varieties
  Japanese eggplant
  Radishes
  Tomatoes, midget varieties
Herbs
  Marjoram
  Rosemary
  Tarragon
  Thyme
Flowering Plants
  Aphelandra
  Cacti and other succulents
  Crossandra
  Dipladenia
  Lobivia
  Lycaste aromatica
  Parodia
  Thunbergia
Foliage Plants
  Any type

West Window
Vegetables
  Lettuce
  Spinach
  Tomatoes
Flowering Plants
  Begonias, especially
   angel-wing
  Bromeliads, especially
   guzmania
  Columnea
  Dendrobium pierardii
  Hoya carnosa
  Kohleria
  Oncidium ampliatum
  Sinningia cardinalis
  Ruellia macrantha
Foliage Plants
  Any type
North Window
Flowering Plants
  Anthurium
  Begonias, especially *rex*
  Bromeliads, especially
   neoregelia, nidularium,
   vriesia
  Campanula
  Gloxinia
  Lantana montevidensis
  Saintpaulia African violets
Foliage Plants
  Dieffenbachia
  Dracaena
  Philodendron

You can even grow mosses and carnivorous plants, projects that are impossible under standard home conditions. However, you may not want to grow trailing plants in the window greenhouse. They take a great deal of space. Large decorator plants belong in the living or dining room, not in the window. So forget that citrus or ficus tree.

Considering all you *can* grow, these exceptions are hardly a loss. Indeed, when you open a window to a greenhouse, you open a door to a new world of gardening.

Growing Conditions—Just what will the conditions be inside your window greenhouse? If the unit is built and installed properly, conditions will be similar to those in a regular greenhouse. Temperature and humidity can be controlled to create ideal growing conditions for almost any plant. Unfortunately, ideal conditions for plants can also mean ideal conditions for insects. You must keep careful watch or insects can take over. But with favorable light, temperatures and humidity, and correct watering, you will be able to have fresh and cheerful greenery and bloom all year long.

Opposite Page
A window greenhouse provides a healthy environment for your plants all year.

Selecting Plants
11

Opposite page
The effect of a well planned small space can easily exceed your expectations.

The following charts include annuals, perennials, shrubs, trees and the beautiful bulbs that can be used in various types of gardens depending on your preference. Because there is are so many plants, the lists that follow are only a sampling.

UNDERSTANDING PLANT NAMES

In the following charts, plants are listed by botanical name, followed by their common name, if there is one. You may think botanical names are confusing, but they are the most exact way to identify plants. Common names change with the times and even with geographic location. A name such as *Juniperus chinensis* 'Pfitzerana', Pfitzer juniper, can be explained as follows. First, *Juniperus* is the plant *genus*. It is capitalized and written in italics. Second, *chinensis*, the plant *species* is written in italics but not capitalized. The third name, which not all plants have, can be a *variety* or *cultivar*. A variety is a plant which occurs naturally but is slightly different from the species. A cultivar is a "cultivated variety" which is propagated or hybridized by plant breeders. Varieties are written in italics and not capitalized. Cultivars are written in normal type, capitalized, and enclosed in single quotes.

MAKING PLANTS WORK FOR YOU

Keep in mind the climate-altering potential of plants. For example, plants are much cooler than pavement. Therefore, for cooler indoor temperatures you should use shrubbery and grass to protect your house or apartment from heat reflected by pavement. Similarly, to protect your house from the sun or to provide an umbrella of shade for plants that need it, choose high arching shade trees. Be sure that low growth

does not prevent air from circulating about the home. Use clinging and climbing vines on trellises to lessen the full blast of the sun in summer. If you plant them against masonry walls they will also provide some insulation from cold in winter.

If you live in an area with very cold winters, consider using deciduous trees, vines and shrubs. In the summer their foliage will screen the hot sun and in winter it will drop and allow the sun to help heat your home.

ANNUALS

Annuals are plants that produce flowers, mature and die in the course of one year. They provide abundant bloom and quick color for any type of garden, and they are inexpensive. You need only to plant and water most annuals to produce their bountiful bloom. If you want color in the garden annuals are indispensible. Some of the best are listed on page 131.

PERENNIALS

Perennials are the backbone of any flower garden. Most of these plants bloom the second year after you plant them and live on for many years. There are perennials for all seasons and in all colors, so you can pick and choose. Most perennials require at least 4 to 6 hours of sun; some will bloom with less light, but not as prolifically.

Perennials need a good porous soil that drains readily. If conditions are good they can take copious amounts of water. They need minimal feeding: perhaps twice a month with a 10-10-5 plant food. For best results, plant perennials in groups of one color to create an accent rather than a conglomerate of color, which can be disturbing to the eye.

Use perennials for easy gardening: they require only one planting and then almost take care of themselves to reward you with bloom year after year.

Perennials are available as prestarted plants at nurseries in season or you can start them from seed. A list of some of the best is found on page 134.

BULBS

Bulbs offer a wealth of beauty for little effort. All you do is plant them. There are dozens of beautiful spring-flowering bulbs and some mighty fine summer types that make any garden a feast of color. They look best planted in drifts of one color where they create a handsome accent. Avoid single row planting because it always looks unattractive.

Basically, all bulbs need a highly organic, but rapid draining soil. They do not grow as well in clay soil and few respond in sandy soil. Dig round holes for bulbs with a concave bottom. This works better than pointed holes that leave air pockets below the bulbs.

The life-cycle of a bulb can be stated as (1) blooming, (2) foliage growth, which is stored in the bulb, (3) flowering, and (4) resting.

Many of the most beautiful bulbs are winter hardy and are left in the ground year after year. They need cold weather to grow. Others must be planted and lifted each year.

Both spring- and summer-flowering types are listed on pages 136 and 137

GROUND COVERS

For ground covers, the soil must be prepared just as if you were planting a lawn. In fact, many ground covers blend harmoniously with grass. Or you may use them simply as lawn substitutes. In general, ground covers require less maintenance than grasses or dichondra. They are not made for heavy use, so think twice if you have small children. Many varieties are listed on page 138.

Combining plants takes careful thought. Consider the total effect when making your choices. You may even want to add a few pumpkins.

VINES

Vines are essential in my gardens. They cover a multitude of sins including cracked walls and unsightly areas, and they create a cascading effect that is very appealing. They screen walls and fences and block out objectionable views. They fit into small spaces and can assume many shapes. Flowering vines are breathtaking in bloom.

Some vines are rampant, others more contained, but almost all need occasional pruning, which can be time consuming. Vines may need more attention than most plants, but they offer so much I suggest you use them in your small space garden. Some of my favorite vines are listed on page 139.

SHRUBS

Shrubs can be a blessing or an eyesore. Too many shrubs will create a jungle look that is rarely attractive. But a few are always desirable because they provide the necessary mass and horizontal lines for an attractive garden. There are flowering shrubs—many pretty ones—and foliage shrubs. The trick is to pick the right ones. Before you make your selections, look over the list on page 144 and the photos throughout this book.

Once planted, shrubs need little attention. They grow almost free of care other than an occasional pruning. Evergreen shrubs are most popular where weather conditions are hospitable. In colder climates, of course, deciduous shrubs are favored because their foliage blocks sun rays in summer and bare branches permit the sun's welcome heat in winter. Shrubs make excellent background plants, but when you put them in place, remember that they need space to grow. A list of some very pretty shrubs is found on page 140.

DECIDUOUS AND EVERGREEN TREES

Trees are the skeleton of any garden, whether it is in the country, in a suburban backyard or on a city roof. A few small trees work wonders to create the total garden plan. There are deciduous trees—those that lose their leaves in winter—and evergreens, which are handsome all year. Deciduous trees offer the benifit of providing shade in summer, but let the sun through in winter. You do have to clean up in fall, however. You should use a combination so there will be color in the garden at all times.

The list of trees is long and varied—some are compact, others bushy, some branching, some columnar and so on. You can create virtually any garden you want. In the lists on pages 144 and 147 we cover both deciduous and evergreen trees.

HERBS

Herbs are treated fully in Chapter 8. A list of the most commonly grown varieties is found on page 148.

Botanical Name Common Name	Approx. Height In Inches	Planting Distance In Inches	Range of Colors	Peak Blooming Season	Location
Antirrhinum majus Common Snapdragon	10 to 48	10 to 18	Large choice of color and flower form	Late Spring and Fall; Summer where cool	Sun
Arctotis stoechadifolia grandis Blue-eyed African Daisy	16 to 24	10	Yellow, rust, pink, white	Early Spring	Sun
Begonia semperflorens cultorum Wax Begonia	6 to 18	6 to 8	White, pink, deep-rose; single or double flowers	All Summer; perennial in temperate climate	Sun or shade
Calendula officinalis Pot Marigold	12 to 24	12 to 15	Cream, yellow, orange, apricot	Winter where mild; late Spring elsewhere	Sun
Centaurea cyanus Bachelor's-button Cornflower	12 to 30	12	Blue, pink, wine, white	Spring where mild; Summer elsewhere	Sun
Clarkia amoena (godetia) Satin Flower	18 to 30	9	Mostly mixed colors; white, pink, salmon, lavender	Late Spring; Summer where cold	Sun
Coreopsis tinctoria Calliopsis	8 to 30	18 to 24	Yellow, orange, maroon, and splashed bicolors	Late Spring to Summer; late Summer where cool	Sun
Delphinium Larkspur	18 to 60	9	Blue, pink, lavender, rose, salmon, carmine	Late Spring to early Summer	Sun
Dianthus Pink	6 to 30	4 to 6	Mostly bicolors of white, pink, lavender, purple	Spring and Fall; Winters where mild	Sun

Dianthus

Begonia semperflorens

Coreopsis tinctoria

ANNUALS

Botanical Name Common Name	Approx. Height In Inches	Planting Distance In Inches	Range of Colors	Peak Blooming Season	Location
Eschscholzia californica California Poppy	12 to 24	9	Gold, yellow, orange; 'Mission Bell' varieties include pink and rose	Winter and Spring in mild climates	Sun
Gaillardia pulchella Rose-ring Gaillardia	12 to 24	9	Zoned patterns in warm shades; wine, maroon	All Summer	Sun
Godetia amoena	See *Clarkia amoena*				
Gypsophila elegans Baby's Breath	12 to 30	6	White, rose, pink	Early Summer to Fall but of short duration	Sun
Helianthus annuus Common Sunflower	36 to 120	3	Yellow, orange, mahogany, or yellow with black centers	Summer	Sun
Helichrysum bracteatum Strawflower	24 to 48	9 to 12	Mixed warm shades; yellow, bronze, orange, pink, white	Late Summer, Fall	Sun
Impatiens balsamina Garden Balsam	8 to 30	9	White, pink, rose, red	Summer to Fall	Light shade; sun where cool
Lathyrus odoratus Sweet Pea	36 to 72	6	Mixed or separate colors; all except yellow, orange, green	Late Winter where mild	Sun
Lobelia erinus Edging Lobelia	2 to 6	6 to 8	Blue, violet, pink, white	Summer	Sun, light shade
Lobularia maritima Sweet Alyssum	4 to 12	12	White, purple, lavender, rosy-pink	Year-round where mild; spring to Fall elsewhere	Sun, light shade

Helianthus annuus

Impatiens balsamina

Eschscholzia californica

Botanical Name Common Name	Approx. Height In Inches	Planting Distance In Inches	Range of Colors	Peak Blooming Season	Location
Matthiola incana Stock	12 to 36	9 to 12	White, cream, yellow, pink, rose, crimson-red, purple	Winter where mild; late Spring elsewhere	Sun
Mirabilis jalapa Four-o'clock	36 to 48	12	Red, yellow, pink, white; some with markings	All Summer	Light shade or full sun
Petunia hybrids Common Petunia	12 to 24	6 to 12	All colors except true blue, yellow and orange	Summer and Fall	Sun
Phlox drummondii Annual Phlox	6 to 18	6 to 9	Numerous bicolors; all shades except blue and gold	Late Spring to Fall	Sun, light shade
Salpiglossis sinuata Painted-tongue	18 to 36	9	Bizarre patterns of red, orange, yellow, pink, purple	Early Summer	Sun, light shade
Tagetes erecta African Marigold Big Marigold	10 to 48	12 to 18	Mostly yellow, tangerine and gold	Generally, all Summer	Sun
Tagetes patula French Marigold	6 to 18	9	Same as African types; also russet, mahogany and bicolors	Early Summer	Sun
Tagetes tenuifolia Signet Marigold	10 to 24	9 to 12	Small; yellow, orange	Generally, all Summer	Sun
Zinnia haegeana Mexican Zinnia	12 to 18	6 to 9	Yellow, orange white, maroon, mahogany	Summer	Sun
Zinnia elegans Common Zinnia	8 to 36	9	Red, orange, yellow, purple, lavender, pink, white	Summer	Sun
Zinnia elegans Youth-and-old-age	12 to 36	12	Same colors as small-flowered common zinnia	Summer	Sun

Tagetes erecta

Petunia

Zinnia elegans

PERENNIALS

Botanical Name Common Name	Approx. Height In Inches	Planting Distance In Inches	Range of Colors	Peak Blooming Season	Location
Althaea rosea Hollyhock	60 to 108	12 to 16	Most colors except true blue and green	Summer	Sun
Alyssum saxatile	8 to 12	12	Golden-yellow tinged with chartreuse	Early Spring	Sun
Anemone coronaria	To 18	12	Red, blue, white	Spring	Sun
Asclepias tuberosa Butterfly Weed	24 to 36	12	Orange	Summer	Sun
Aster, dwarf type	8 to 15	8 to 12	Red, blue, purple	Late Summer	Sun
Campanula carpatica Tussock Bellflower	8 to 10	12	Blue, white	Summer	Sun
Campanula persicifolia Willow Bellflower	24 to 36	9	White, blue, pink	Summer	Sun
Chrysanthemum coccineum Painted Daisy Pyrethrum Daisy	24 to 36	12	White, pink, red	Early Summer	Sun
Chrysanthemum maximum Daisy Chrysanthemum	24 to 48	12	White	Summer, Fall	Sun or shade
Chrysanthemum morifolium Florist's Mum	18 to 30	12 to 18	Most colors except blue	Late Summer, Fall	Sun
Coreopsis grandiflora	24 to 36	18	Golden yellow	Summer	Sun
Delphinium hybrids	24 to 36	12	Blue, violet, white	Early Summer	Sun
Dianthus barbatus Sweet William	10 to 30	9	White, pink, red; zoned and edged	Early Summer	Sun or light shade
Felicia amelloides Blue Daisy Blue Marguerite	20 to 24	12	Blue	Spring, Summer	Sun
Gaillardia grandiflora	24 to 48	12	Yellow or bicolor	Summer, Fall	Sun
Gazania hybrids	10 to 12	6	Yellow, gold, orange & white	Summer, Fall; Spring where mild	Sun

Dianthus barbatus, see also page 129.

Felicia amelloides

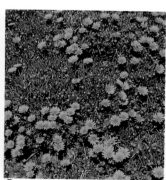

Gazania, Yellow trailing

Botanical Name Common Name	Approx. Height in Inches	Planting Distance in Inches	Range of Colors	Peak Blooming Season	Location
Gypsophila paniculata Baby's Breath	24 to 36	24	White	Early Summer and Summer	Sun
Helenium Sneezeweed	24 to 48	12	Orange, yellow, rusty shades	Summer, Fall	Sun
Hosta plantaginea Fragrant Plantain Lily	24 to 30	20	White flowers, yellow-green leaves	Late Summer	Light shade
Iris, various types	3 to 10 (dwarf); 15 to 28 (intermediate); 24 to 48 (tall)	20 12 16	Numerous colors	Spring, early Summer	Sun or light shade
Iris cristata Crested Dwarf Iris	6 to 8	10	Lavender, light blue	Spring	Light shade
Kniphofia, various types Poker Plant Red-Hot Poker Torch Lily	24 to 72	18	Cream, white, yellow, orange	Early Summer	Sun
Liatris pycnostachya	60 to 72	12	Rose-purple	Summer	Sun or light shade
Lobelia cardinalis Cardinal Flower Indian Pink	24 to 36	9	Red	Late Summer	Sun, light shade
Rudbeckia hirta Black-Eyed Susan	36 to 48	12	Yellow, pink, orange, white	Summer	Sun
Salvia patens Gentian Sage	24 to 36	12	Dark blue	Summer, Fall	Sun
Scabiosa caucasica	24 to 30	12	White, blue, purple	Summer, Fall	Sun
Solidago Goldenrod	20 to 36	12	Yellow	Summer	Sun or light shade
Veronica Speedwell	24 to 36	6	Blue, pink, white	Mid-Summer	Light shade
Viola cornuta	6 to 8	6	Purple; newer varieties in many colors	Spring, Fall	Light shade
Yucca filamentosa Adam's Needle	36 to 72	36	White	Late Summer	Sun

Gazania 'Copper King'

Hosta plantaginea

Viola cornuta 'Purpurea'

SPRING-FLOWERING BULBS

Botanical Name Common Name	When to Plant	Planting Depth in Inches	Location	Remarks
Allium Onion	Fall	3	Sun	Ornamental varieties are prettier than you might expect.
Chionodoxa Glory-of-the-Snow	Fall	3	Sun	Do not disturb for several years. Thrives in any soil, but needs plenty of moisture and light.
Convallaria majalis Lily-of-the-Valley	Fall	3	Light shade	Forms dense clumps. Hardy outdoors. Will last for years.
Crocus	Fall	3 to 4	Sun	Always dependable. Dig up bulbs every 3 or 4 years after leaves die down, store and replant in September.
Eranthis Winter Aconite	Early Fall	3	Shade	Very early bloom. Thrives in most places.
Erythronium Adder's Tongue Dog-Tooth Violet Fawn Lily Trout Lily	Early Fall	3 to 5	Shade	Good for natural appearance, especially in rock gardens. Needs well-drained soil.
Fritillaria Fritillary	Fall	4	Shade	Overlooked but lovely. Easy to cultivate.
Galanthus Snowdrop	Fall	3 to 4	Shade	Blooms while snow is on the ground. Hardy and easy.
Hyacinthus Hyacinth	Fall	6 to 8	Sun	Protect from wind and mice. Hardy. Needs well-drained soil. Mulch in winter.
Leucojum Snowflake	Fall	3	Shade	Flowers last a long time. Hardy. Leave bulbs in soil for several years.
Muscari Grape Hyacinth	Early Fall	3	Sun	Easy to grow. Attractive in groups.
Narcissus Daffodil Jonquil	Fall	6	Sun	Every member of this genus is called Daffodil. They are hardy outdoors and fit in with local flora. Best to lift bulbs every few years.
Scilla Squill	Fall	2	Sun or light shade	Once established, blooms indefinitely. Hardy.
Tulipa Tulip	Fall	4 to 6	Sun or light shade	Dozens of varieties and forms. Needs fertile, well-drained soil. Mulch in winter.

From left to right:
daffodils with hyacinth
tulips
scilla.

SUMMER-FLOWERING BULBS

Botanical Name Common Name	When to Plant	Planting Depth In Inches	Location	Remarks
Agapanthus africanus Lily-of-the-Nile African Lily	Spring	1	Sun	Grows to 20 inches tall, but new dwarf varieties are available. Deep violet-blue, funnel-shaped blossoms.
Alstroemeria Lily-of-the-Incas Peruvian Lily	Spring	4	Partial shade	Good cut flowers. Not hardy. Needs to be stored over winter. Good in pots.
Caladium Mother-in-Law Plant Elephant's Ear Angel-Wings	Spring	4	Shade	Lovely foliage plants for either pots or bedding. Many varieties. Start tubers in boxes with rich loam with bonemeal added. Prefers warm climates.
Canna	Spring	2	Sun	Showy flowers; lift rhizomes after frost kills tops and do not replant until threat of frost is past. Many varieties: most are hybrids. Likes moist soil with high humus.
Dahlia	Early Spring	6	Sun	Many varieties and forms. Needs water and fertilizer.
Galtonia candicans Summer Hyacinth	Spring	6	Sun	Buy new bulbs yearly. Does best in rich, moist soil.
Hemerocallis Daylily	Spring	3	Sun	Flowers profusely. Thrives in almost any soil condition.
Iris Flag Fleur-de-Lis	Depends on variety	1	Sun	Dozens of varieties. Some can be forced indoors.
Lilium Lily	Depends on variety	6	Light shade	Many varieties and forms, usually easy to grow. Prefers light, sandy soil.
Polianthes tuberosa Tuberose	Late Spring	1	Sun	Plant after danger of frost. Store in warm, dry place over winter.
Ranunculus Buttercup	Depends on variety	1	Sun	Lovely colorful flowers. Store tubers in dry place over winter.
Sprekelia formosissima Jacobean Lily St. Jame's Lily Aztec Lily Orchid Amaryllis	Spring	3	Sun	Good in pots. Store bulbs in dry place over winter.
Tigridia Tiger Flower Shell Flower One-Day Lily	Late Spring	2 to 3	Sun	Store bulbs in dry place before first frost. Seed sown in Spring will bloom the following year.
Tritonia	Late Spring	2 to 3	Sun	Hardy except for far north, can be left in ground.
Zephyranthes Zephyr Lily Rain Lily Fairy Lily	Spring	1	Sun or light shade	Hardy outdoors with winter protection. Store bulbs over winter in very cold climates.

From left to right:
Iris
hemerocallis
ranunculus
dahlia

GROUND COVER PLANTS

Botanical Name / Common Name	Location	Description
Ajuga reptans Carpet bugle	Partial shade	Fast growing plant with dark green foliage reaching to 4 inches. Blue flower spikes appear in spring.
Cotoneaster	Full sun	Shrubby, with small leaves and decorative berries. Vigorous grower. Low maintenance.
Dichondra micrantha Dichondra	Sun or light shade	Often grown as a lawn in mild winter areas. Miniature cup-shaped leaves form a continuous, dark green mat.
Epimedium	Partial shade	Semi-evergreen, with glossy leaves and red, pink, white or light yellow flowers.
Hosta Plantain Lily	Shade	Some varieties have large heart-shaped leaves, others have small leaves. Buy in full leaf to be sure you get what you want. Dormant in winter.
Iberis sempervirens Evergreen Candytuft	Full sun	Dense little bushes with white flowers.
Liriope spicata Creeping lilyturf	Sun or partial shade	A low, clumping grasslike plant, reaching 10 to 12 inches in height. Very hardy.
Lonicera japonica 'Halliana' Hall's Japanese Honeysuckle	Sun or shade	Tough rampant vine. Flowers are white, but change to yellow.
Mesembryanthemum crystallinum Ice Plant	Full sun	Stiff leaves and bright daisy-like flowers. Slow spreading. Hardy.
Pachysandra terminalis Japanese Pachysandra, Japanese Spurge	Shade	Whorls of dark green leaves. Spreads on underground runners.
Rosmarinus officinalis Rosemary	Full sun	Narrow leaves and blue flowers in spring. Stands hot sun and poor soil. Drought tolerant.
Sagina subulata Irish moss	Sun or partial shade	Looks much like moss. Deep green in color. *S. subulata* 'Aurea' is a yellowish green.

Clockwise from above:
Pachysandra terminalis
    with *Ilex cornuta*
Cotoneaster horizontalis
Lonicera japonica 'Halliana'

Botanical Name Common Name	Length In Feet	Location	Remarks
Akebia quinata Five-Leaf Akebia, Chocolate Vine	to 25	Sun or partial shade	Vigorous twiner; fragrant small flowers.
Ampelopsis brevipedunculata Blueberry Climber	to 20	Sun or shade	Strong grower with dense leaves.
Aristolochia durior Dutchman's Pipe, Pipe Vine	to 30	Sun or shade	Big twiner with mammoth leaves.
Clematis armandii Evergreen Clematis	Depends on variety	Sun	Lovely flowers and foliage.
Euonymus fortunei	to 20	Sun or shade	Shiny, leathery leaves; orange berries in fall.
Hedera helix English Ivy	Depends on variety	Shade	Scalloped neat leaves; many varieties.
Hydrangea anomala petiolaris Climbing Hydrangea	to 70	Sun or partial shade	Heads of snowy flowers.
Ipomoea purpurea Morning-Glory	to 50	Sun	Flowers are white, blue, purple, pink or red.
Lonicera japonica 'Halliana' Hall's Japanese Honeysuckle	to 25	Sun or shade	Deep green leaves, bronze in fall. Also a good ground cover.
Parthenocissus quinquefolia Virginia Creeper	to 30	Sun or shade	Scarlet leaves in fall.
Pueraria thunbergiana Kudzu Vine	to 60	Sun or partial shade	Purple flowers. Very invasive.
Rosa Rose	Depends on variety	Sun	Many climbing varieties with a wide range of colors.
Thunbergia alata Black-eyed Susan Vine	to 6	Sun	Perennial in mild climates. Likes heat.
Wisteria floribunda Japanese Wisteria	to 35	Sun	Violet-blue flowers.

Clockwise from left:
Clematis armandii
Parthenocissus quinquefolia
Wisteria floribunda
Hedera helix

SHRUBS

Botanical Name Common Name	Approximate Height In Feet	Lowest Night Temperature	Location	Remarks
Abelia grandiflora Glossy Abelia	5	−10°F (−23°C)	Sun	Free flowering in Summer. New growth is bronze. Protect from wind. Evergreen.
Abeliophyllum distichum White Forsythia	3 to 4	−10°F (−23°C)	Sun	Prune after bloom in early Spring. Deciduous.
Andromeda polifolia Bog Rosemary	1 to 2	−50°F (−45°C)	Sun or partial shade	Likes moist locations. Good in rock gardens. Evergreen.
Berberis koreana	2 to 10	−10°F (−23°C)	Sun	Outstanding colored flowers; red berries. Deciduous.
Berberis thunbergii Japanese Barberry	7	−10°F (−23°C)	Sun	Grows in any soil. Red berries appear throughout Winter. Deciduous.
Buddleia alternifolia Fountain Butterfly Bush	12	−10°F (−23°C)	Sun or partial shade	Graceful; branching. Clusters of purple blossoms. Does well in poor soils. Deciduous.
Buddleia davidii Common Butterfly Bush Orange-Eye Bush Summer Lilac	15	−10°F (−23°C)	Sun or partial shade	Many varieties. Fast growth. Freezes back, but roots are hardy. Flowers in Fall. Attracts butterflies. Deciduous.
Buxus microphylla japonica Japanese Boxwood	4	−10°F (−23°C)	Sun or shade	Low and compact. Evergreen but looks poor in cold Winters.
Buxus microphylla koreana Korean Boxwood	6 to 10	−20°F (−28°C)	Sun or shade	Hardiest boxwood; tolerates alkaline soil. Foliage turns brown in Winter.
Carpenteria californica Bush Anemone Tree Anemone	8	5°F (−15°C)	Sun or shade	Showy white flowers in Summer Slow growing. Evergreen
Euonymus alata Winged Euonymus	9	−35°F (−37°C)	Sun	Sturdy, easily grown. Leaves turn red in Fall. Deciduous.
Euonymus japonica Evergreen Euonymus Japanese Euonymus Spindle Tree	15	10°F (−12°C)	Sun	Splendid glossy foliage. Stands heat and poor soil. Watch for mildew.

Buxus microphylla japonica

Abelia grandiflora

Botanical Name Common Name	Approximate Height In Feet	Lowest Night Temperature	Location	Remarks
Euonymus latifolia	20	−10°F (−23°C)	Sun	Vigorous grower. Hardy.
Forsythia intermedia Border Forsythia	2 to 9	−20°F (−28°C)	Sun	Deep yellow flowers in Spring. Deciduous.
Forsythia ovata	8	−20°F (−28°C)	Sun	Earliest to bloom and hardiest. Not particular about soil. Vigorous growth.
Fothergilla major	9	−10°F (−23°C)	Partial shade	Good flowers and autumn color. Likes long, hot Summers.
Gardenia jasminoides Cape Jasmine	4 to 6	10°F (−12°C)	Sun or shade	Fragrant white blossoms. Needs warmth. Water often. Evergreen.
Hamamelis vernalis Witch Hazel	10	−10°F (−23°C)	Sun or shade	Yellow flowers in early Spring; yellow leaves in Fall. Deciduous.

Hydrangea arborescens
  Hills-of-Snow
  Wild Hydrangea
	3	−20°F (−28°C)	Partial shade	Easy culture. Dense growth with large flower clusters. Deciduous.

Ilex cornuta
  Chinese Holly
  Horned Holly
	9	5°F (−15°C)	Sun	Lustrous foliage, bright berries. Needs long, warm season for fruit to set. Evergreen.

Ilex crenata Japanese Holly	20	−5°F (−20°C)	Sun or shade	A good holly with black berries Many varieties. Evergreen.
Jasminium nudiflorum Winter Jasmine	15	−10°F (−23°C)	Sun or partial shade	Viny shrub; not fragrant. Does well in cooler climates. Needs clipping.

Jasminium officinale
  Common White Jasmine
  Poet's Jessamine
	30	5°F (−15°C)	Sun or partial shade	Grows tall. Semi-evergreen to deciduous.

Juniperus chinensis 'Pfitzerana' Pfitzer Juniper	6	−20°F (−28°C)	Sun	Popular juniper. Gray-green needles. Do not overwater. Evergreen.

Kalmia latifolia
  Calico Bush
  Mountain Laurel
	30	−20°F (−28°C)	Partial shade	Showy flowers; slow growth. Needs regular watering, acid soil.

Forsythia ovata

Hydrangea arborescens

SHRUBS

Botanical Name Common Name	Approximate Height In Feet	Lowest Night Temperature	Location	Remarks
Mahonia aquifolium Holly Mahonia Mountain Grape Oregon Grape	3 to 5	−10°F (−23°C)	Sun or shade	Handsome foliage looks good all year. Drought tolerant. Evergreen.
Pieris floribunda Fetterbush Mountain Pieris	5	−20°F (−28°C)	Partial shade	Does well in dry soil. Needs acid conditions. Protect from wind. Evergreen.
Pieris japonica Lily-of-the-Valley Bush	9	−10°F (−23°C)	Partial shade	Splendid color; new growth is red. Protect from sun and wind. Water often. Evergreen.
Potentilla fruticosa Golden Hardhack Shrubby Cinquifoil	2 to 5	−50°F (−45°C)	Sun	Many varieties. Hardy. Blooms from June to November.
Rosa species Brier Rose	2 to 4	−20°F (−28°C)	Sun or shade	Dozens of different types and varieties. Select one suited to your climate.
Spiraea arguta	6	−20°F (−28°C)	Sun	Free flowering. Needs water. Deciduous.
Spiraea prunifolia Bridal Wreath Spiraea Shoe Button Spiraea	9	−20°F (−28°C)	Sun or partial shade	Graceful form. Small leaves turn orange in Fall. Deciduous.
Spiraea thunbergii	5	−20°F (−28°C)	Sun or partial shade	Arching branches; small white flowers in April. Deciduous.
Spiraea veitchii	12	−10°F (−23°C)	Sun or partial shade	Good background shrub; Deciduous. Graceful form; white flowers.

Juniperus pfitzerana 'Aurea'

Ilex cornuta 'Burfordii'

Botanical Name Common Name	Approximate Height In Feet	Lowest Night Temperature	Location	Remarks
Syringa villosa Late Lilac	9	−50°F (−45°C)	Sun	Dense, upright habit. Lilac or pinkish white flowers. Deciduous.
Syringa vulgaris Common Lilac	20	−35°F (−37°C)	Sun	Many varieties. Needs period of dormancy to bloom well. Deciduous.
Viburnum davidii	3	5°F (−15°C)	Partial shade	Handsome leaves; bloom not showy. Likes acid soil. Evergreen.
Viburnum dentatum Arrowwood	15	−50°F (−45°C)	Sun or shade	Red Fall color. Will stand either moist or dry soil. Deciduous.
Viburnum opulus European Cranberry Bush Whitten Tree	12	−35°F (−37°C)	Sun	Good many varieties. Showy flowers; large red fruit. Watch for aphids. Deciduous.
Viburnum prunifolium Black Haw Sheepberry Sweet Horn	15	−35°F (−37°C)	Sun	Good specimen plant. Showy flowers, leaf color in Fall. Deciduous.
Viburnum sieboldii	30	−20°F (−28°C)	Sun	Stellar performer. Hardy. Deciduous.
Viburnum trilobum Cranberry Bush Highbush Cranberry	12	−50°F (−45°C)	Sun	Attractive in Winter. Red fruit, Fall color, small white flowers. Deciduous.
Weigela florida	9	−10°F (−23°C)	Sun or partial shade	Many varieties available. Fast growth. Red funnel-shaped flowers. Not very attractive without bloom. Deciduous.

Euonymus japonica

Syringa vulgaris

DECIDUOUS TREES

Botanical Name / Common Name	Approximate Height In Feet	Lowest Night Temperature	Remarks
Acer platanoides Norway Maple	90	−20°F (−28°C)	Grows rapidly; dense foliage. Hardy. Purple-leafed varieties available.
Acer rubrum Red Maple Scarlet Maple	80	−20°F (−28°C)	Rapid growth; red leaves and fruits. Red flowers in late Spring. Likes sandy soil.
Aesculus carnea Red Horse Chestnut	40	−20°F (−28°C)	No autumn color; hardy.
Ailanthus altissima Copal Tree Tree-of-Heaven Varnish Tree	60	−10°F (−23°C)	Very adaptable; resists smog and insects.
Albizia julibrissin Mimosa Silk Tree	20	−10°F (−23°C)	Very ornamental; likes high temperature in Summer. Pink flowers; fern-like leaves. Messy.
Betula pendula European White Birch	60	−30°F (−34°C)	Graceful but short-lived. Bark is white and flakes off in layers.
Carya ovata Shagbark Hickory Shellbark Hickory	120	−10°F (−23°C)	Slow growth; narrow upright habit. Nuts are edible.
Celtis occidentalis Nettle Tree Sugarberry	120	−35°F (−37°C)	Good shade tree; hardy when established. No surface roots.
Cercis canadensis Redbud	40	−10°F (−23°C)	Lovely pink flowers. Hardiest redbud.
Chionanthus virginicus Old-Man's-Beard	30	−10°F (−23°C)	Bountiful flowers in late Spring. Needs sunny location, loamy soil.
Cornus florida Eastern Dogwood Flowering Dogwood	40	−10°F (−23°C)	Spring bloom; red berries; leaves turn in Fall; many varieties.
Cornus kousa Kousa Dogwood	20	−5°F (−20°C)	Lovely flowers in June. Hardy.

Acer rubrum

Cornus kousa

Cornus florida

DECIDUOUS TREES

Botanical Name Common Name	Approximate Height In Feet	Lowest Night Temperature	Remarks
Crataegus mollis Downy Hawthorn	35	−10°F (−23°C)	A large hawthorn with pear-shaped fruit.
Fagus grandifolia American Beech	120	−20°F (−28°C)	Excellent ornamental tree.
Fagus sylvatica European Beech	80	−10°F (−23°C)	Several varieties; spreading branches can reach ground.
Koelreuteria paniculata Goldenrain Tree Varnish Tree	30	−5°F (−20°C)	Magnificent yellow Summer bloom. Hardy tree. Tolerates alkaline soil. Needs sunny location.
Laburnum watereri Golden-Chain Tree	25	−5°F (−20°C)	Deep yellow flowers. Hardy.
Liquidambar styraciflua Red Gum Sweet Gum	70	−5°F (−20°C)	Beautiful symmetrical cone shape; bright Fall foliage.
Magnolia soulangiana Chinese Magnolia Saucer Magnolia	25	−5°F (−20°C)	Many varieties; also evergreens, shrubs; large flowers.
Magnolia stellata Star Magnolia	25	−5°F (−20°C)	Very ornamental; profuse bloom.
Malus baccata Siberian Crabapple	45	−35°F (−37°C)	Lovely white flowers; red and yellow fruit. Hardy.

Magnolia soulangiana

Ailanthus altissima

Cercis canadensis

DECIDUOUS TREES

Botanical Name Common Name	Approximate Height In Feet	Lowest Night Temperature	Remarks

Malus floribunda
   Purple Chokeberry
   Showy Crabapple
	25	−10°F (−23°C)	Handsome foliage and red, pink or white flowers. Hardy tree.

Populus alba
   Silver-Leaved Poplar
   White Poplar
	90	−20°F (−28°C)	Wide-spreading form makes good windbreak. Rapid growth; hardy. Roots can be invasive.

Salix alba White Willow	40	−35°F (−37°C)	Good upright willow. Does well in moist location.
Salix babylonica Weeping Willow	40	−5°F (−20°C)	Fast grower; needs plenty of water.

Tilia americana
   American Linden
   Basswood
   Whitewood
	130	−35°F (−37°C)	Fragrant white flowers in July; compact shape. Hardy, but not drought tolerant.

Tilia cordata
   Littleleaf Linden
   Small-Leafed Linden
	100	−20°F (−28°C)	Dense habit. Hardy, but not drought tolerant.

Tilia tomentosa Silver Linden	80	−10°F (−23°C)	Beautiful pyramid-shaped specimen tree. Fragrant bloom in Summer.

Ulmus americana
   American Elm
   White Elm
	120	−35°F (−37°C)	Popular shade tree; hardy. Suckers can be a problem. Highly susceptible to Dutch Elm disease. Spray yearly for insects.

Clockwise from top left:
Liquidambar styraciflua
Tillia cordata
Salix babylonica
Populus alba
Albizia julibrissin

Botanical Name Common Name	Approximate Height In Feet	Lowest Night Temperature	Remarks
Abies balsamea Balsam Fir Fir Balsam	75	−35°F (−37°C)	Handsome ornamental. Prefers cool growing season. Not smog resistant.
Cedrus atlantica Atlas Cedar	60	−5°F (−20°C)	Slow growth; nice pyramid shape; seldom needs pruning. Prefers sheltered location.
Chamaecyparis obtusa Hinoki Cypress Japanese False Cypress	120	−20°F (−28°C)	Broadly pyramidal. Hardy in northern climates.
Juniperus virginiana Red Cedar	50	−50°F (−45°C)	Slow growth; cone shape; hardy. Red winter foliage.
Pinus bungeana Lace-Bark Pine	75	−20°F (−28°C)	Slow growing. Flaky bark.
Pinus densiflora Japanese Red Pine	80	−20°F (−28°C)	Flat-top habit. Can be damaged by severe winter.
Pinus nigra Austrian Pine	100	−20°F (−28°C)	Fast growing.
Pinus parviflora Japanese White Pine	50	−10°F (−23°C)	Handsome ornamental.
Taxus baccata English Yew	60	−5°F (−20°C)	Best among yews. Densely branched. Foliage is poisonous if eaten.
Taxus cuspidata 'Capitata' Japanese Yew	50	−20°F (−28°C)	Good landscape tree. Spreading or upright form.
Thuja occidentalis American Arbovitae White Cedar	60	−50°F (−45°C)	Leaves dark green on top, yellow-green on bottom; sometimes turn brown in winter.
Tsuga canadensis Canada Hemlock	80	−35°F (−37°C)	Dense form has many uses; hedges, screens. Best when protected from winter sun and wind.
Tsuga caroliniana Carolina Hemlock	70	−20°F (−28°C)	Fine all-purpose evergreen; soft looking.
Tsuga diversifolia Japanese Hemlock	50	−10°F (−23°C)	Smaller than most hemlocks. New branches are reddish-brown.

Pinus nigra

Chamaecyparis obtusa

HERBS

Botanical Name Common Name	Type	Height In Inches	Planting Distance In Inches	Location	Uses
Allium schoenoprasum Chive	Perennial	18	6	Full sun	Cuttings for salads, egg dishes, soups or with sour cream on baked potatoes.
Anethum graveolens Dill	Annual	36	In Clumps	Full sun	Seeds for pickling; leaves for soup, salad, fish or lamb.
Anthriscus cerefolium Chervil	Annual	18	6	Partial shade	Leaves for fish, soups and salads.
Armoracia rusticana Horseradish	Perennial	15	12	Full sun	Root used as a condiment or appetizer with meats.
Artemisia dracunculus Tarragon	Perennial	24	12	Full sun	Leaves for salads, poultry, fish, egg and cheese dishes.
Borago officinalis Borage	Annual	36	15	Full sun	Leaves for salads or drinks.
Chamaemelum nobile Chamomile	Perennial	12	4	Full sun	Whole herb for tea.
Coriandrum sativum Coriander Chinese Parsley	Annual	24	12	Partial shade	Seeds in baking; leaves as flavoring for salad dressings or meat.
Crocus sativus Saffron	Perennial bulb	12 to 18	3	Full sun; protect from wind	Stigmas for taste and color in many dishes.
Cuminum cyminum Cumin	Annual	12	6	Full sun	Seeds used in curries or pickling.
Levisticum officinale Lovage	Perennial	48	36	Partial shade	Leaves for soups; seed in biscuits or with meat.
Melissa officinalis Balm, Lemon Balm	Perennial	12 to 18	18	Partial shade	Leaves used like mint with fish or meat, in salads or drinks.
Mentha crispa Curled Mint	Perennial	12	12	Partial shade	Leaves for salads, drinks or to make tea or sauce.
Mentha piperita Peppermint	Perennial	20 to 24	8	Full sun	Leaves for jelly and as garnish.
Mentha spicata Spearmint	Perennial	12 to 20	6	Full sun	Leaves in sauces, jellies, beverages and as garnishes.
Mentha suaveolens Apple Mint	Perennial	12	12	Partial shade	Leaves for salads, drinks or to make tea or sauce.

Chamaemelum nobile

Petroselinum crispum

Armoracia rusticana

Botanical Name Common Name	Type	Height In Inches	Planting Distance In Inches	Location	Uses
Monarda fistulosa Bergamot	Perennial	4 to 24	8	Partial shade	Leaves for tea.
Nasturtium officinale Watercress	Perennial	4 to 24	In Clumps	Full sun in water	Shoots for salads, soups or as garnish.
Ocimum basilicum Sweet basil	Annual	18	6	Full sun	Leaves for soups, salads, fish and meat.
Ocimum minimum Basil	Annual	24	10	Full sun; protect from wind	Leaves for soups, meat, fish and vegetables.
Origanum majorana Sweet marjoram	Annual	10	4 to 6	Full sun	Leaves for meat.
Petroselinum crispum Parsley	Biennial, but grown as Annual	10 to 15	6	Partial shade	Cuttings for vegetables, salads, soups, stews or as garnish.
Pimpinella anisum Anise	Annual	18	6	Full sun	Leaves for salads, seeds for baking.
Rosmarinus officinalis Rosemary	Perennial	36	18	Full sun	Leaves for soups, stews or chicken.
Salvia officinalis Sage	Perennial	24	15	Full sun	Leaves with meats, fish or in stuffing for poultry.
Satureja hortensis Summer savory	Annual	12 to 18	5	Full sun	Leaves in stew, meat loaf, pork or fish.
Satureja montana Winter savory	Perennial	6 to 16	6	Full sun	Leaves for salami.
Thymus Thyme	Perennial	12	8	Full sun	Leaves with meat, fish, vegetables, soups or stuffing.

Allium schoenoprasum

Thymus

Basic Gardening

12

All the gardening chemicals that flood the market—foods, fertilizers, insecticides—are not totally necessary. No, gardening on your scale, in small spaces, is *not* highly "scientific" and does *not* involve constant attention. You can still pretty much garden naturally as Grandma did; that is, just use a good soil, select your plants intelligently, and supply enough water to plants. However, some chemicals are necessary, as we have learned since Grandma's time. Soil nutrients do get depleted and you have to "inject" the elements back into the soil via fertilizers. Insects can run rampant to the point that only a poison will kill them. But overall, gardening is still fairly easy and rewarding, believe me. You will have to spend only a minimal amount of money on a few commercial products. Generally, let nature help you through organic mulches, natural watering—rain—and predators like birds, which love to eat insects. You do *not* have to kill yourself cultivating the beautiful garden; wise planning, nature, and a few chemicals are your happy co-workers.

SOIL

There is so much talk about soils that it is a wonder people have enough courage to just start a garden in the plain old dirt outside their homes. But be brave—I have started many gardens on spent soil, adding a few chemicals, only a few, as I went. Eventually, although never overnight, I created a lovely garden.

Soil is the basis of practically all gardening. Only when the soil is properly prepared can you start to grow plants. Generally, existing soil in the small garden is depleted of nutrients because it has been used many years. Or, it is a new site where good top soil has been bulldozed away leaving only subsoil.

Earth or garden soil has two layers: topsoil and subsoil. The subsoil is beneath the surface layer; it has been there for hundreds of years, and it can be a few inches below the surface or as much as 20 inches down. The subsoil varies greatly in composition and can be sandy or clayey. A very sandy subsoil will retain little moisture and is useless for plants. Subsoil that is very clayey will hold water so long that plants, literally drown in it. It should be broken up, or in severe cases, a drainage system may have to be installed to carry off water.

Topsoil is composed of small particles of disintegrated rock, minerals and decomposing organic matter. In addition, it contains living organisms, such as bacteria and fungi, and water which holds the dissolved mineral salts and air. Most soils lose their mineral content over the years, and the soil must be reworked and revitalized. The layer of topsoil is generally a darker color than the deeper subsoil because of organic content.

TYPES OF SOIL

There are three basic kinds of soil: clay, which is heavy; a sandy soil, which is light; and a loamy soil, which is porous. A heavy clay soil is difficult to work with. It is slow in drying out in the spring, does not absorb the sun's heat as readily as a lighter soil and so does not

warm up in the spring as quickly as eager new plants demand. The very small particles of clay have tiny air spaces that tend to compact, making it difficult for water or air to penetrate. Frequently, a clay soil forms a crust that makes it impossible for air or water to reach the roots of plants. You must add humus and sand to it to improve clay soil's structure. The amount you use depends on the density or size of the mineral particles of your particular soil.

Sandy soil contains larger particles that permit a freer passage of water and air. Sandy soil is easy to work with and warms up quickly in spring, but it does not retain moisture or provide good drainage. And many of the soluble plant foods will be lost through *leaching*, which is the removal of salts or impurities by water seeping through the roots. Adding liberal quantities of organic matter will improve a sandy soil.

Loamy soil is a fertile mixture of clay, sand and *humus*. It is porous in texture and provides good drainage, yet it is spongy, so it retains moisture. This is the kind of soil we want in our garden. But in most cases, it must be developed by a program of soil conditioning.

Humus—Decayed organic, matter such as animal manure, compost, leaf-mold or peat moss are sources of humus. Humus refers to living organisms and their remains which have decayed. Humus adds body to light soils and provides aeration for clay soils. It dissolves in the soil and provides nourishment for plants and micro-organisms essential for plant nutrition. It is constantly consumed and depleted in this process and must be replaced. Maintenance of the proper proportion of humus in the soil is vital to good plant growth.

A good general rule for adding humus to soil is to mix in about 1 inch of humus to about 6 inches of soil. This should create porosity and get the micro-organisms moving to enrich the soil.

A convenient source of humus is peat moss, which is available at nurseries. While there are differences between the various types of peat available, through the years I have used many kinds and they all proved satisfactory. A second source of humus is leafmold, which is composed of decayed leaves and grass clippings. It is easy to make and you can usually find it free. To make your own leafmold, simply rake leaves into a pile and let them decompose. Another excellent source of humus is compost, and this too is free. It is basically decayed vegetable matter.. Leaves, grass clippings, dead twigs and such also can be added.

Even if you add humus to the soil, you will also have to use fertilizers to supplement it as discussed on the next page. But fertilizers are not substitutes for humus, nor can decayed organic matter do the work of fertilizers. Your garden soil will need both.

Drainage System for Clay Soils— As mentioned above, good drainage is essential to prevent soggy soil which can harm plants. If you cannot improve the physical structure of a clay soil by turning it and adding humus, then by all means be sure to have drainage facilities put in place. This will help the problem but not solve it completely. You will have to dig deep ditches—about 36 inches deep and install a 2-inch bed of coarse gravel and lay appropriate drain tiles available at suppliers. This will help to pull off most of the excess water.

Water—A good soil has excellent water absorption. Moisture is transported quickly through pores in the soil to the roots of the plant where it is stored for future use. The pores also carry away excess water. so that the topsoil does not become soggy. Once soil is waterlogged, air is prevented from circulating freely —a necessary factor for good plant growth.

Drainage—Good drainage is essential to prevent waterlogging, which can kill plants. This condition causes the plants to develop shallow roots. The plants then perish from a lack of moisture because they cannot reach down for the stored water below. Poor drainage is a common fault of most soils and is generally caused by a layer of hard earth. This condition can be natural, and can occur at almost any depth. But most often it is caused during construction by housing developers who tamp down soil by driving trucks and other heavy equipment over it. Because this compacted soil, or *hardpan*, can be underneath the surface, you should test your soil with a soil sampling tube. The tube is simply pushed into the ground to the depth you choose. Twist and remove the tube and it will hold a column of earth that will tell you the composition of each layer in the proposed gardening areas. The gray section will be hardpan. The light gray will be sub soil and the black-gray will be topsoil. Soil-testing kits are available at many nurseries.

Porosity—Plant roots need oxygen, so soil must be porous. It should be crumbly and have an coarse texture so that provisions for air and water are perfect. Air enters the soil as the water drains through the soil.

Improve the physical structure of the soil by turning it, keeping it porous and using composts and mulches throughout the year. Porosity is the key to good soil. Only when the little air passages are in the soil is it worthwhile to fertilize and work your garden. Fertility alone will not give good plant growth. The physical condition or *tilth* of the soil is just as important in the overall working of the soil.

As soon as you are in your new home, dig up some soil and crumble it in your hand. If it is lumpy and clayey, you will need to add the necessary sand and humus. If it is sandy and falls apart in your hand, you will need to add some organic matter. A good soil crumbles between the fingers. It feels like a well-done baked potato—porous with good texture.

If you must buy your garden soil, remember there are dozens of kinds. Get a *screened* soil with all the necessary additives—this is expensive—from a *reputable* dealer. If you need large amounts, you can buy it by the truckload. Soil comes in 6-yard trucks and is delivered *tailgate* to your home. This means that the truck just dumps it on your property. You have to spread the soil yourself. You can buy smaller amounts of soil in 50- or 100-pound sacks.

pH SYMBOL

Most plants thrive in a *neutral* soil, one that is neither too alkaline nor too acidic. But some plants prefer either an acid or an alkaline soil. The pH of a soil incidates whether there is acidity or alkalinity; soil with a pH of 7 is neutral. Below 7 is acid, and above 7 is alkaline. Determine your soil's pH by testing with a commercial soil-testing kit.

To lower the pH of your soil—that is, to increase the acidity—add 1 pound of ground sulfur per 100 square feet. This lowers the pH reading about 1 point. To raise or *sweeten* the pH, add 10 pounds of ground limestone per 150 square feet. Sulfur or limestone should be applied several times or at six to eight week intervals.

FEEDING

Most gardeners pour out their affection for their plants in the form of plant foods, also called fertilizers. But in some cases, such as with nasturtiums, too much feeding can stop plants from blooming, so use plant foods discriminately. If your soil has the necessary nutrients, a lot of feeding will not be necessary. Feed annuals or perennials twice a month, trees and shrubs once a month. Too much food will not kill your plants, it will just wash away, so don't waste your money.

COMMERCIAL FERTILIZERS

Commercially made plant foods contain certain percentages of nutrients. These percentages are marked on the package as, for example, 10-10-5. The first number indicates *nitrogen*, in this case 10 percent. Nitrogen makes plants grow. The second number indicates *phosphorus*, again 10 percent. Phosphorus promotes strong stems and leaves. The last number, 5, indicates 5 percent *potassium* or *potash*. Potash helps plants resist disease. The other 75 percent of the mix is filler which may contain small amounts of elements such as iron.

For most plants a 10-10-5 food formula is ideal, neither too strong nor too weak. However, fertilizers specially made for specific plants, such as roses, are sometimes better than all-purpose foods. For example, to make plants bloom, use a food with high phosphorus content, like 12-12-12 or 5-10-5. If you want something to improve the soil structure and release nutrients slowly, use an organic food like blood meal or bone meal.

There are five types of synthetic fertilizers you can buy. Here's a rundown on them:

● **Powdered**—Good, but it blows away on windy days. It may stick to foliage and, if stored in a damp place, it will cake.

● **Concentrated liquids**—Easy to use—just dilute with water. Suitable for all types of plants.

● **Concentrated powders**—Easy to use but should be applied only to foliage and roots.

● **Concentrated tablets**—Used mostly for houseplants. Can be dissolved in water or put directly into the soil and allowed to dissolve gradually as you water plants.

● **Pellets or granular**—Easy to spread and the easiest form to use. Some granular fertilizers also contain insecticides or weed killers.

There are also materials that contain nitrogen you can use to help plants grow. Quick-releasing nitrogen materials act immediately and are water-soluble. But they do not last long, so frequent light applications are necessary for uniform growth over a long period of time. Ammonium sulfate, ammonium nitrate, urea, nitrate of soda, ammonium phosphate and calcium nitrate are among the quick-releasing materials.

Slow-releasing nitrogen materials depend upon soil bacteria for their decomposition and transformation into the nitrogen forms that then become available to the plant. There are two groups of materials that slowly release nitrogen into the soil. They are organic matter and ureaform compounds. Organic matter includes many substances, such as sewerage sludge, animal and vegetable tankage, manures and cottonseed meal. Ureaform compounds are synthetic materials made by a chemical union of urea and formaldehyde. Do not confuse *urea*, which contains quick-releasing nitrogen, with *ureaform*.

WATERING

Most people really water only the surface of the soil, so the roots never get the water. When you water, saturate the soil for more than 3 hours. In 3 hours water penetrates soil just a few inches. Plant roots are usually deeper than a few inches, so light waterings are not enough. This dictum about watering is especially important for flowering plants and vegetables, which demand buckets of water.

WHEN AND HOW MUCH

The adage that you should water early in the morning before the sun gets too hot isn't gospel. True, this advice can't hurt plants, but I water at all times of the *day* and have yet to harm a single plant. Avoid watering at night, because then the soil retains too much moisture. And if the night temperature is very cool, fungus may form in the soil.

Rainfall may take care of most of your watering, but during very hot days or in areas of drought or low rainfall, help your plants with additional watering. Water annuals, perennials, and vegetables every day during June, July and August. You can skip a day now and then, but only now and then—otherwise you will not get flowers or produce. Shrubs, vines and trees need less water than flowers, but, of course, they should never be bone dry.

CLIMATE

Your region's climate determines how much water and food plants need and what you can and cannot grow. In warmer climates there is more sun, and the sun's intensity determines how much food plants can assimilate and how much water is needed. If you are new in a neighborhood, ask neighbors about the climate and look at their gardens. And remember that nearby areas can have completely different climatic differences. In California, areas only 3 or 4 miles apart have wide climatic variation. Also, get some rainfall and average sunlight maps of your area from the U.S. Department of Agriculture, Office of Information, Washington, D.C. 20250. These maps will tell you more than reams of written information.

MULCHING

Mulching is the spreading of various materials, usually organic, between and around plants to cover the soil. It is one of the most important gardening techniques. Mulching decreases the amount of moisture lost through evaporation, keeps the soil cool, helps minimize harmful effects of thawing and freezing, and helps control weed development because weeds don't have room to grow easily under a protective coating. If possible, keep plants mulched year round, but be sure to add new mulch after the soil has warmed up in spring and growth has started. If you apply mulches too early, growth will stop because the soil will still be cool.

Mulches can be composed of such nonorganic materials as aluminum foil, roofing paper, stones, and gravel. But for best results, use one of these six organic mulches:

- **Leaves**—Old oak leaves or pine needles make an acid mulch, but they should be shredded first.
- **Hay, straw**—Perfect organic mulches because they decompose slowly and are weed-free.
- **Grass clippings**—Mix clippings with a coarse material to prevent matting. Beware of Bermuda grass clippings because they may take root.
- **Cocoa beans, pecan shells**—Cocoa beans and pecan shells decompose slowly, but they are alkaline. Do not use them around acid-loving plants.
- **Ground fir bark**—Fir bark, available in several grades, is an

PREPARING YOUR SOIL

Turning your soil with a spade will make it more porous and easy to work. Add any soil amendments you may need.

Keep turning the soil, even after you have added humus, sand or even new top soil.

Rake the soil into a finished bed. It should be porous and mealy to the touch.

extremely good mulch because it decomposes slowly, is attractive, and stays in place.

• **Sawdust, wood chips**—Beware: these mulches draw nitrogen out of the soil and may harbor ticks.

CULTURE

If you are an inexperienced gardener, you may unintentionally be the cause of some plant problems. For example, you may not water plants thoroughly or you may allow too much wind to buffet the plants. You may have placed sun-loving plants in the shade, or vice versa.

Here are some tips for the "uncultured" gardener.

Brown spots or crisply edged leaves or new growth that quickly withers indicate too much heat and fluctuating soil temperatures. New leaves that are yellow may lack acidity. However, leaves that turn yellow and drop off may do so naturally. Brown or silvery spots on leaves mean too much sun. And if leaves look lifeless, they are not getting enough water.

Buds will suddenly drop off plants if temperatures fluctuate too much—there is no remedy. Plants that do not bloom as they should are not getting enough sun. And stems that turn soft and leaves that wilt are in too much shade with too much moisture.

INSECTS

Inspect all plants before planting them to make sure there are no bugs in the soil. And keep your garden clean to avoid insects: Throw away trash because insects often hide in it, and cut and burn dead wood because insects nest in it.

If you see some insects, don't panic. Many insects are harmless and actually help control the vicious and damaging sucking and chewing varieties. For example, the lacewing fly eats harmful plant lice. Ladybugs eat aphids, nasty bugs that can decimate a plant and often bring ants with them. Praying mantises

eat hundreds of bugs daily. Tachina flies nourish themselves with cutworms and caterpillars. And digger wasps and wheel bugs eat the larvae of unwelcome insects.

On the other hand, damaging insects may invade your garden. Sucking-type bugs pierce plant tissue; chewing-type insects eat various plant parts. Some insects attack any plant; others prefer specific plants such as roses. Most insects are easy to spot, but some tiny ones are almost invisible and thus the most difficult to control. Hard-to-see insects include root lice, mites and stem borers.

BIOLOGICAL CONTROL

This method fights nature with nature by using the natural enemies of insects rather than poisons. These include birds, other insects, mulching, and certain plants, such as onions and marigolds, which repel insects. As noted previously, ladybugs, praying mantises, lacewing bugs and others are all part of the organic gardener's arsenal. Swallows eat many types of insects, and purple martins feed on wasps, flies and other insects. Martins nest in communities, so give them a birdhouse. Kingbirds eat aphids and caterpillars at ground level or catch insects while flying. The Baltimore oriole eats caterpillars, pupae and adult moths. Wrens, titmice and bushtits are other birds that will help keep your garden almost insect-free.

On the other hand, English sparrows, linnets, house finches and mockingbirds can eat your berries and other fruits, so try to keep these birds out of your garden.

This is gardening without chemicals and without disturbing the balance of nature. Grandma would be delighted to see you working with nature, rather than against it.

INSECTICIDES

I recommend insecticides *only* when all else fails. There are numerous insecticides on the market, often

sold by chemical rather than generic name. Insecticides are classified as either inorganic, botanical or synthetic. Arsenic is inorganic but generally no longer in use. *Pyrethrum* and *rotenone* are botanical preventatives because they are derived from plants. Synthetic insecticides include chlorinated hydrocarbons, carbonates and organophosphates. Do *not* use the hydrocarbon-types; *chlordane, lindane* and *aldrin* because they are highly poisonous to humans.

Other commonly used insecticides include *derris, malathion, petroleum oil* and *tar oil.*

Apply insecticides when insects are most vulnerable—in the early stages of their life or just after they have hatched from their eggs. You can kill most sucking insects by applying contact poisons directly to their bodies. Kill the chewing insects by applying poisons to the plant parts being attacked. Insects eating stems or leaves containing insecticide die of internal poisoning.

Insecticides can be sprayed, dusted or spread. Use a sprayer attached to a hose or a portable sprayer and you should be able to reach all parts of plants. Spray in the early morning or late afternoon because hot sun on sprayed plants sometimes harms them. Be sure the ground is wet before spraying. After spraying, wash the sprayer thoroughly with soapy water and rinse carefully with clean water. Read the product label.

Dusting is messy, and if you dust on a windy day, you can get the poison in your lungs. Dusts are applied dry as they come from the package. Usually the poison is a very small percentage of the total mixture. Compared to spraying and spreading, dusting often is the thriftier method of application.

Spreading, the easiest way to kill insects, is fast and clean. Just sprinkle insecticide on the ground and water the soil.

SYSTEMIC POISONS

Another popular insecticide is a type called *systemic*. Systemic poisons are absorbed by the plant roots, and all parts of the plant become toxic to many, but not all insects for 4 to 6 weeks. This type of poison is especially important for the elimination of certain aphids such as greenflies, which are immune to insecticides applied to the plant externally. Systemic poisons become part of the sap of the plants rather than remaining outside where they are applied.

Why Use Them?—It is advantageous to use systemic poisons because they are long lasting and kill only harmful insects, not those that provide beneficial services to the plant. On the other hand, they are so toxic to human beings that they should be used only if absolutely necessary.

Systemic poisons come in granular form, such as *Meta-systox-R*. The granules are sprinkled on the ground and then water is applied. Systemic insecticides also are available in a soluble liquid such as *Benomyl,* which must be mixed with water. Both types are easy to apply. Use with extreme caution and strictly according to directions on the package.

DISEASES

Many destructive plant diseases are caused by fungi, bacteria and viruses. There are thousands of different kinds of fungi: rot, wilt, rust and powdery mildew are caused by fungi. Bacteria are microscopic organisms that live in soil or plant parts and cause blights, rot, wilting, galls, fire blight and iris rhizome rot, but not all bacteria are bad. Many of the most serious diseases of ornamental plants are caused by viruses, and these remain a mystery. If your plant looks sick, take it to your nursery to identify the disease. The wrong treatment can also kill a plant.

Poor plant care often invites diseases. A poorly cared-for plant, like a human being in poor health, is more susceptible to attack by disease. Insects also spread diseases from one plant to another. Fungi and bacteria are most responsive to moisture and temperature. Excessive moisture in the soil can lead to root rot and plants in shade are more likely to develop diseases.

Nurseries carry many types of young plants in trays. Choose carefully and be sure to allow for growth when you buy. Too many plants will create a jungle rather than a garden.

PREVENTING DISEASES

Diseases can attack any plant, but a well-cared for garden will rarely be attacked—plants are just too healthy and conditions such as soil, moisture will not be conducive to disease. However, if a disease does start in the garden there are preventatives. There are chemical preparations specifically compounded to thwart fungus and other diseases. *Captan* and *Zineb* are two of the most popular fungicides. These are available at your nursery.

If you need to use fungicides in the garden, be sure to follow package directions carefully and keep all chemicals out of reach of children and pets.

PLANTING

I know it is difficult to determine how many plants for a specific garden, so only general guidelines can be given here. What you want is a garden with enough space between plants so they can grow. Avoid crowding and creating a jungle effect. It is better to start with fewer plants than you might want because you can always add plants later if the garden seems sparse.

The basic techniques of putting plants in the ground are touched on in many garden books, but the actual planting of perennials and annuals, shrubs and trees needs more description. It is wise to remember that a properly planted shrub or tree will have a better chance of surviving than one shallowly or improperly planted.

Trees, shrubs and many vines require deep planting holes to grow readily. First, condition the soil as previously described; then dig down at least 14 to 18 inches and scoop out soil to a diameter of, say, 20 inches. This may seem like a trench but it is not. Trees and shrubs need good root space. If you are working with *bare root* plants, spread out the roots in the hole. Then fill in with soil, tamp down and firm the soil around the *collar* of the plant, the area where the stem joins the roots. Bare root shrubs or trees are deciduous and are sold during their winter dormancy without soil around their roots. Soaking their roots for a few hours before planting will encourage healthy growth. Water thoroughly after the shrub or tree is planted.

If you are planting shrubs or trees that are *balled and burlapped,* or *B and B,* cut the twine but leave the burlap in place. Place the plant in the hole, fill in and around with soil and water thoroughly. In time the burlap will decay and add humus to the soil. *B and B* refers to the *ball* or dirt around the roots, and to the *burlap* wrapped around it.

Whatever you are planting, always try to get the new plants into the ground as soon as possible. Allowing plants to remain without soil can harm them and lessen the chances of a successful planting.

When working with *prestarted* perennials or annuals, plants that have already begun growing in containers, be sure the soil is ready for the plants. It should be crumbly and porous so the seedlings have a chance to grow. Hard clay soil can not accept water, it runs off. Sandy soil drains so quickly the little plants cannot get moisture. Spade and till the soil to aerate it. If the area has been extensively gardened, add some fresh topsoil so plants will have adequate nutrients. Impoverished soil will only support a plant, not give it adequate nutrients to grow. If you cannot afford new topsoil or do not want to add it, at least enrich the

First, clear a hole in the top soil. The depth of the hole depends on the size and type of plant you are planting.

Wet the prestarted plant and remove it from the pack by pressing on the bottom until the plant falls out.

Place the plant into the hole and cover the base of the plant. Pat the soil firmly around the roots.

The freshly planted plant should stand upright on its own. Leave enough space between plants to allow for growth.

Shrubs are usually sold in metal cans. It is best to have the can cut at the nursery so the plant can be removed without damage.

Set the shrub in a hole that is deep enough to allow it to sit at the same level to the surface of the soil as it was in its can.

soil with some compost or humus comprised of decayed leaves, twigs or lawn clippings. This will supply essential nutrients to your plants.

When planting perennials and annuals, dig down at least 6 inches, scoop out a pocket of soil and take the new plant with root ball intact, if possible, and place it in the hole. Push in soil and tamp down gently. Add enough soil to reach around the collar of the plant and then water thoroughly. If you are planting your own seedlings the same rules apply.

TRANSPLANTING

Transplanting is moving a grown or partially grown plant from one location to another and it involves careful handling. You cannot just pull a plant out of the ground, replant it, and expect it to grow. The shock could kill the plant. If you decide to move a plant to another location, first dig down around the plant, but be careful not to cut off roots as you spade into the soil. If the plant is a shrub or tree, it is best to do this job during cool weather. About three days before you move the plant, saturate the roots with water so they will hold together better. When you transplant, dig around the shrub or tree at or near the *drip line,* an imaginary line under its outermost branches where it sheds rainwater. Retain sufficient soil around the roots to preserve the greatest amount of the root structure. if you are working in sandy soil, wrap burlap around the root ball and fasten it with twine or wire. More compact soils hold together well and generally don't require burlap. If the shrub or tree is large, be sure to have someone handy to help you transport it to the new site where the soil should already be prepared as if for a new planting.

If you are transplanting something smaller, dig around the perimeter of the plant and remove about 2 to 3 inches of soil. Jiggle the plant and tease it from the original position. Do not tug it loose. Keep

jiggling it back and forth until it comes out freely. Then remove some of the old soil from the root ball and trim way any dead roots. Dead roots are brown. Then prepare the new planting hole as described previously for new plantings, and transplant.

PRUNING

Pruning and trimming plants are part of a good garden program. Pruning shapes plants, allows free circulation of air and light, directs growth, and removes dead or injured parts. It also increases the quality or yield of fruits or flowers.

The kind of pruning needed varies at different times in the life of the plant. Many trees and shrubs must be cut back somewhat severely at planting time to insure that there will be strong new growth. Some ornamental trees and most fruit trees must be pruned to grow properly. All fruit trees require some pruning. Vines and some trees and shrubs need training to make them handsome.

WHERE AND HOW TO CUT

It is important to know where to make a cut when pruning. Indiscriminate butchering must be avoided. Cut only above a bud or a small side branch or a main branch. Do not leave a small stub; it will wither and die and is an invitation to both insects and decay. Cut branches in the direction you want the new growth to take. If you need vertical accent for the garden design, keep the lower branches pruned. However, remove them only after they have served their purpose in nourishing the tree or shrub. If you are trying to shape a plant to a pattern, trim away twiggy and unattractive growth so the well-placed branches can be seen.

SHADE TREES

Young shade trees need pruning to help them develop a strong framework that resists wind. Remove unwanted branches before they be-

come formidable. Trim out crossed branches; these give a tree an unkempt appearance. If one branch grows faster than others, prune it when it is young to keep the tree shapely.

Large trees are best pruned by a professional. Special equipment and skill are necessary when cutting heavy limbs. It is hazardous work and it is wiser to pay a tree service fee than a hospital bill. Shade trees usually are trimmed in summer, but if the temperature is not too low, they can be cut at any time.

In all pruning—but especially with shade trees—never leave a stub. Cut branches flush with the trunk. And cover all cuts with tree wound solution, available at nurseries.

DECIDUOUS FLOWERING SHRUBS AND TREES

On some deciduous shrubs and trees, old branches bloom while current or new wood blossoms on others. Before pruning deciduous shrubs and trees, find out whether they flower on old or new wood. Shrubs that bloom on previous years' wood in spring or early summer can be pruned immediately after they flower. Cut away weak shoots, unattractive branches, and old flowering stems. The idea is to allow light and air to the plant so that new flowering branches can grow. If you prune shrubs and trees in spring or winter, only thin them.

Pruning is important for both shrubs and trees. It encourages new growth, but take care not to cut too much.

Index